Sadlier-Oxford
STUDENT
GUIDES

Writing a Research Paper
A Step-By-Step Approach

Phyllis Goldenberg

Program Consultant

J. Forrest Tucker
Technology Coordinator
St. Luke's School
New York, NY

Sadlier-Oxford
A Division of William H. Sadlier, Inc.

Acknowledgments

The publisher wishes to thank the following individuals for their suggestions for, and contributions to, the original edition of *A Student Guide to Writing a Research Paper*.

Curriculum Reviewers

Frederick J. Panzer
Christopher Columbus High School
Miami, Florida

Patricia Stack
South Park School District
Library, Pennsylvania

Paul David Rivadue
Garden City High School
Garden City, New York

Thomas Pasko
Saint Ignatius High School
Cleveland, Ohio

Student Reviewers

Michael Dinger
Garden City, New York

Elizabeth O'Donnell
Yardley, Pennsylvania

Cynthia Dinger
Larchmont, New York

Cartoon Research by Photosearch, Inc: pages 7, 42, 66, 95, 107, 122, 133

Ten Steps to a Successful Research Paper

The new edition of *Writing a Recearch Paper* maintains the unique, step-by-step approach of the original: It encourages students to complete their papers as they complete the book. It also introduces two new features—**E-writing** and **Online Research**—that acknowledge the role that computers now play in both the research for and the writing of student papers.

At each step students are introduced to a key element of the process, then given exercises to help them practice and master that element, and finally prompted to apply it to or incorporate it in their own research papers.

In content and method *Writing a Research Paper: A Step-by-Step Approach* is designed to be equally useful to those students who are writing a research paper for the first time and those who have many such papers behind them. For first-time writers this book provides a clearly organized plan—from choosing the topic to submitting the finished paper—as well as a wealth of practical advice. For more experienced writers the book will prove a handy review and reference manual, complete with reminders, cautions, and hints to help assure better-planned and better-written papers.

Special Features

NEW! **E-writing** Practical suggestions for writing on a computer

NEW! **Online Research** Helpful hints for getting the most out of Internet research

Hint! Useful advice meant to facilitate the research paper process

Cartoons Chapter openers focusing on the lighter side of the writing process

TIMETABLES Suggested schedules for completing the project

APPENDICES Three supplements providing information on reference materials, topic ideas across the curriculum, and alternate formats and styles.

☑ **Checklist Review**
End-of-chapter recaps

Contents

Preface

By the time you finish this book, you will have transformed blank sheets of paper into a coherent, fact-filled, smooth-sounding research paper that you can be proud of. In the process, you will become a local expert on the topic you have chosen to write about. You will probably end up knowing a great deal more about your topic than any of your classmate, friends, or family. What you find out about your topic will stay with you a long, long time.

That's the *content*—the information you discover.

Research also involves a *process*—how you go about finding information.

Think of this book as a tool kit and map combined in one handy package. It will give you all the tools—the essential skills—you will need in order to plan and complete your research paper, and it will guide you—that's the map part—every step of the way. Literally, you will complete ten steps in the research process.

As you research and write, you will be working some of the time with a partner or with a small group. You and your classmates will advise and support each other as you compare notes on your progress and discoveries and comment on one another's work.

If this book belongs to you, keep it. No matter how many research papers you are asked to write in the future, the steps of researching and writing will be the same. The content of your future papers will change, but the process will remain the same.

Are you feeling curious? nervous? impatient to begin? You're only ten steps away from your finished research paper, so step right up for Step 1—boot up the computer and have a great time!

Phyllis Goldenberg

Choose a Topic

PEANUTS reprinted with permission of UFS, Inc.

So you have to write a research paper. You have just been handed one of the most interesting—and challenging—writing assignments of your school career. To complete the assignment on time, you will need to begin promptly and keep plugging away until you have finished. So let's get started! The first thing you will need to do is decide what you are going to write about.

Before You Begin

☑ **Make sure you understand your assignment.**

A research paper is a long, formal essay or report that presents information from a number of sources. You will need to know exactly when your paper is due, how long it is supposed to be, and what type of research paper you are expected to write.

LENGTH. Your teacher may specify a paper ranging in length from 1,000 to 2,000 words (sometimes more). You can estimate 250 typed words to a double-spaced page to determine the number of pages of text you will need. Or your teacher may assign a specific number of pages—5 to 7 double-spaced pages of text, for example. Listen carefully to the assignment, and follow the specifications (for length, topic, type of paper, style of documentation) exactly.

Keep in mind that whenever you write a report, explain an idea, or write a memo or proposal, your writing is **expository** in nature; that is, your purpose is to inform or explain. You are not telling a story (**narrative** writing) or **describing** something or trying to convince someone to do something (**persuasive** writing). In expository writing, your purpose is chiefly to convey information to your reader.

AUDIENCE. Usually your teacher and your classmates are your audience, but some-times a research paper can be shared with others who are interested in your topic. For instance, if you have written a paper about a strong-mayor versus a city-commis-sion form of government, you might read and discuss your paper with a government class or send it to your local governing body. If you have written about recent legislation protecting an endangered species, you might share your findings with the school's science club or a local environmental organization.

TYPES OF RESEARCH PAPERS. Research papers, which are sometimes called *term papers*, can be classified as either **informational** or **analytical**.

An informational paper summarizes factual information from a variety of sources. The writer's task in such a paper is to focus the topic, find the information, and produce an organized and coherent paper. A paper that explains how hybrid cars work would be informational.

An analytical, or *evaluative*, paper goes one step further. In this kind of paper, the writer analyzes the information and presents his or her conclusions. Because it states the writer's opinion and supports it with detailed evidence, an analytical research paper displays some of the elements of persuasive writing. A paper that presents three reasons why hybrid cars are good for the environment would be analytical.

Make sure you understand whether your teacher wants an informational paper or an analytical paper.

Managing Your Time

☑ Draw up a project schedule.

A research paper is a long-term assignment. In order to see it through to a successful conclusion, you will need to plan and keep to a schedule. Indeed, one of the most important aspects of a research paper project is time management—that is, making the most efficient use of the time available to you.

Your teacher will specify a deadline (the date on which your paper is due). You then have from the day the paper is assigned until the due date to research and write it. Therefore, your first order of business should be to draw up a project schedule. The sample timetables on page 9 give you some guidelines on how to pace yourself.

AVOID A TIME TRAP. Some teachers may require that you turn in specific materials along the way—for example, an outline or a list of sources. Such mini-deadlines can actually help you stay focused on your task. Other teachers may assign the research paper, give you some specifications and a due date, and then leave you on your own. In that case, it's completely up to you to manage your time. Don't procrastinate. The due date may seem a long way away, but you've got lots of work to do.

KEEP PLUGGING AWAY. Don't get bogged down in one stage of the writing process, such as writing a thesis statement. If you keep plugging away at your assignment, you will be able to meet your deadline.

Research Paper Timetables

The chart below gives four timetables, each keyed to a different assignment span, that you might use as models to adopt or adapt, as best suits your own research paper.

STEPS	10 weeks	8 weeks	6 weeks	4 weeks
PREWRITING				
1 Choose a topic	1 week	3 days	2 days	1 day
2 Locate sources	3 days	3 days	2 days	1 day
3 Take notes	2 weeks	$1\frac{1}{2}$ weeks	1 week	1 week
4 Write a thesis statement and a title	3 days	2 days	1 day	1 day
5 Write a final outline	1 week	1 week	2 days	2 days
DRAFTING				
6 Write the first draft	$1\frac{1}{2}$ weeks	1 week	1 week	4 days
7 Document sources	2 days	2 days	1 day	1 day
REVISING				
8 Revise	2 weeks	$1\frac{1}{2}$ weeks	$1\frac{1}{2}$ weeks	3 days
PROOFREADING				
9 Proofread	2 days	2 days	2 days	1 day
10 Prepare the final manuscript	3 days	3 days	3 days	2 days

Choosing a Topic

IF A SPECIFIC TOPIC IS ASSIGNED. Be grateful and get going. Rarely, however, does a teacher require everyone to write on the same topic. When more than one person is working on a specific topic, source materials become hard to find because several people are competing for them. Also, most teachers prefer reading about a variety of topics instead of the same one over and over.

IF THE GENERAL SUBJECT IS ASSIGNED BUT NOT THE SPECIFIC TOPIC. If your teacher assigns a general subject and lets you limit it to a workable topic, part of your job is already done. Limiting is easy once you get started. (See pages 12–14 for examples of and suggestions for cluster diagrams.)

IF IT'S TOTALLY UP TO YOU. This is the usual scenario: Your teacher lets you decide what to write about and simply requires that he or she approve your topic once you have chosen it. It is important to settle on a workable topic as soon as possible because you have a lot of work to do once you have made your choice and had it approved. (See Appendix B for suggestions for topics that might interest you.)

Hint!

You don't have to find the "perfect" topic (it probably doesn't exist anyway). You just have to find a *workable* one.

☑ **Choose a workable topic that meets all the following requirements.**

1. YOU CAN FIND ENOUGH MATERIAL ON THE TOPIC. Usually, a research assignment calls for at least five diverse sources, some print and some nonprint. Sometimes, for instance, you will be expected to conduct an interview to serve as one of your sources. Avoid choosing a topic that is too recent or too technical; you will have trouble locating information. Once you have chosen a topic, do a quick check in your library or media center (see Step 2) to verify that you can find five or more reliable sources on it.

2. THE TOPIC INTERESTS YOU, AND YOU THINK YOU CAN MAKE IT INTEREST YOUR AUDIENCE. An ideal topic tickles your curiosity. You may know something about it already, but you would like to know more. After all, you are going to spend many weeks immersed in the topic. Ask yourself if you would like to become the class "expert" on this topic.

Take an interest inventory. Start by taking stock of the things you are interested in. List as many as possible. For example, you might include your hobbies; your ambitions and goals; careers you are interested in; places you would like to visit; things you are curious about (ideas; how something works and why); the biggest problems in your community, the country, the world; things you would buy if you had all the money you wanted; ten famous people you admire and a word or two about why you admire each.

Look for topic ideas. Explore as many sources as you can for possible research paper topics. Browse through newspapers and magazines. Talk to relatives, friends, experts. Interview someone. Listen to radio talk shows, National Public Radio, news shows. Watch TV documentaries and the evening news. Browse through the documentary section of a video store. Browse through a library or bookstore. Check out electronic magazines and newspapers on a computer. Flip through an encyclopedia. Use a search engine to browse for topics on the Internet.

Exercise 1 Brainstorm

Alone or with a partner or small group, brainstorm topics that interest you. On a separate sheet of paper or your computer, make a list of ideas and suggestions, including those that you gathered in your interest inventory. Then review the list, and choose the three topics you would most like to write about.

3. THE TOPIC IS OBJECTIVE, NOT SUBJECTIVE. An objective topic is factual, not personal. Generally, in a research paper you are not writing about your opinions, your experiences, your friends and relatives, or your feelings and ideas. These are subjective topics. Here are some examples of each type:

* **OBJECTIVE** Evidence for and against side airbags in cars

* **SUBJECTIVE** My uncle's car accident

* **OBJECTIVE** Signing up voters: techniques for registering new voters

* **SUBJECTIVE** What happened when I tried to register to vote

4. THE TOPIC IS LIMITED ENOUGH TO BE COVERED ADEQUATELY IN THE SPACE AVAILABLE TO YOU. You will need to focus your topic until it's just the right size. You can't, for example, write a research paper on the history of China; you would need a whole book or several—to cover such a broad subject. Limit, or narrow, your topic to one that can be covered thoroughly in the space you have available. (On pages 12–17, you will learn some techniques for limiting a general subject.) But do not choose a topic so narrow that you can cover it completely in a paragraph or two.

Hint!
If you can find several books devoted to your topic, the topic is too broad and general and needs to be limited further. For example, if you choose to write about Native American mythology and find six books on that subject listed in your library's catalog, your topic needs to be narrowed further.

* **TOO GENERAL** Ants

* **STILL TOO GENERAL** Fire ants

* **STILL TOO GENERAL** The evolution of fire ants

* **JUST RIGHT** The invasion of fire ants in the United States

* **TOO LIMITED** What to do if you are stung by a fire ant

* **TOO LIMITED** What a fire ant looks like

Use a search engine to browse through the listings on a general topic. (A *search engine* is an Internet resource that searches for Web pages containing information about a specified topic.) If you enter the word *karate*, for instance, a search engine will provide hundreds of listings, and they will all be more limited in some way than the general word *karate*. Here are some examples of more limited topics:

history of	USA Karate Foundation
training and equipment	other international karate foundations
rules and etiquette	Karate Hall of Fame
how it differs from other martial arts	karate competitions

Clustering

A **cluster diagram** is a doodle with a purpose, a graphic device for limiting a general subject to workable topics. Start by writing the big idea—a broad, general subject—in the middle of a piece of paper, and circle it. Then break the big idea into its parts or into smaller ideas or topics you associate with it. Write each smaller idea, circle it, and draw a line connecting it to the center. Keep going, writing still more limited topics branching outward. Here is an example:

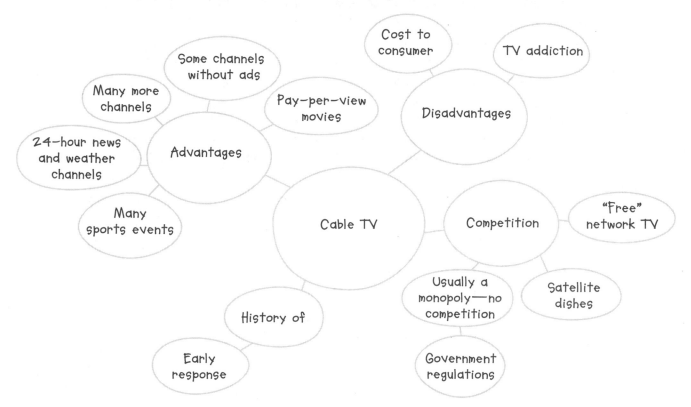

Making a Cluster Diagram

In the space below, fill in a cluster diagram of one of the topics you came up with in Exercise 1. Remember, there are no right or wrong clusters. Start with the topic in the middle and branch out from there. Keep going until you run out of ideas and/or room. Add more circles if you need them.

disadvantages

Facebook Topic

not doing anything you shouldn't be

advantages

STRAIGHT-LINE CLUSTER. A straight-line cluster is another kind of diagram that will help you limit a broad topic. It moves from a broad, general subject (at the top) to ever more limited, narrower topics. Try it. You may find it more useful than the bigger cluster.

French Impressionist Painting

↓

Paintings of Claude Monet

↓

Monet's series of paintings of same subject

↓

Monet's Haystack Paintings 1888–1891

Hint!

Your cluster diagram may look entirely different from those of your classmates, even though you all might start with the same broad, general subject. There are no "right" topics in a cluster diagram. A cluster records your own thoughts as you move from a general idea to narrower topics.

Fill in the straight-line cluster diagram here. Start with a general topic and keep limiting it further and further. Your topic should move from the general at the top to the more and more limited as you approach the bottom. On a separate sheet of paper or your computer, make at least two more of these diagrams, starting each one with a different topic.

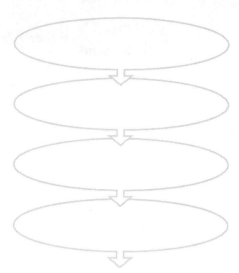

Research Questions

☑ **Word your limited topic as a research question that you are going to investigate.**

Before you start exploring possible sources of information, spend a few minutes jotting down what you already know—or think you know—about your topic. This will help focus your research still further. As you take notes or freewrite, you may end up with one or more research questions—questions to which you would like to find the answers.

TAKING NOTES. Here are some notes made by a student writer for a paper on reforms in the jury system in U.S. courts. The student wrote down everything she already knew and ended by focusing on the research question she wanted to explore.

> Courts use juries in trials to decide whether a person is innocent or guilty as accused. Both criminal and civil. Are there always 12 jurors?
>
> Juries are supposed to be "jury of peers"—a mix of people who represent the population—of ages, races, gender. Are juries mentioned in U.S. Constitution?
>
> How are people called to serve on juries, and what is the source of their names? I think maybe the lists of registered voters or in some places everyone with a driver's license. How old do you have to be?
>
> Who actually gets to choose jurors—the lawyers? the judge?—and how are they chosen?
>
> Cases of innocent people being convicted and guilty people going free.
>
> I'd like to research proposed reforms (changes) in jury system. How can I find out?

FREEWRITING OR QUICKWRITING. Another way to find out what you already know is to freewrite or quickwrite for a few minutes. Keep yourself focused on your topic, and just start writing. Don't worry about complete sentences or connections between ideas. The point is simply to get what's in your brain on paper or onto your computer monitor. Freewriting may contain information as well as questions. Because you think much faster than you write, use abbreviations, fragments, or anything else to capture your thoughts as you focus on your topic.

> Research key words "jury reform" through a search engine and on InfoTrac. See if I can interview Tony's mom, assistant state district attorney. I can write to natl or state Bar Assoc (organization of lawyers) & ask for info about jury reform. Maybe talk with Ben's older brother— graduated from law school last year & was editor of law review. Ask him for advice on how to research the topic—what are best sources?

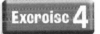

Identifying Appropriately Limited Topics

For each numbered item below, identify the topics that are neither too general nor too limited but just right for a 5- to 7-page research paper. Write the letter of the topic you picked, and explain why you did not pick the others.

1. **a.** The population of the United States
   b. Information from the latest U.S. census
   c. Some problems in collecting accurate information In the latest U.S. census
   d. The number of people of Vietnamese origin living in San Francisco, according the latest census

   _____

   _____

   _____

2. **a.** Symbolism in Robert Frost's "Stopping by Woods on a Snowy Evening" and "Mending Wall"
   b. Robert Frost's poetry
   c. Symbolism in contemporary American poetry
   d. The origin of the word *wall*

   _____

   _____

   _____

3. a. Careers in medicine

   b. Pros and cons of being a nurse in a hospital emergency room

   c. The history of medicine in Europe during the twentieth century

   d. Medical research today

_____

_____

_____

4. a. The career of Jackie Robinson, the first African American baseball player in the major leagues

   b. African Americans and baseball

   c. The history of baseball in America

   d. The World Series

_____

_____

_____

5. a. U.S. presidential elections

   b. Pros and cons of paid political advertisements

   c. How the U.S. presidential candidates are chosen

   d. Problems with various types of voting machines

_____

_____

_____

6. a. Harriet Tubman's accomplishments on the Underground Railroad

   b. History of slavery in the Americas

   c. Fugitive slave laws

   d. *Roots* by Alex Haley—tracing the writer's origins back to Africa

_____

_____

_____

7. a. The history of writing

   b. Cracking hieroglyphics—the Rosetta stone

   c. Cuneiform and hieroglyphics—precursors of the alphabet

   d. Sequoya's invention of an alphabet for the Cherokee language

_____

_____

_____

8. a. History of and current requirements for physical education classes in local schools

   b. Overweight Americans

   c. Too much TV

   d. Health benefits of sports and other forms of exercise

_____

_____

_____

 Limiting a Broad Subject

See how many limited topics appropriate for a research paper you can list for each of the broad, general subjects below. Use a separate sheet of paper or your computer. Here is an example to get you started.

General topic. Dogs

Limited topics. Obedience training; breeds of dogs that are good with children; crime-fighting dogs; how seeing-eye dogs are trained; most dangerous dogs; animal shelters; rabies and other serious diseases; from wolves to dogs—their early history

1. Popular music	**6.** Circuses
2. Space travel	**7.** Television
3. Cartoons	**8.** Careers in science
4. World War II	**9.** Community problems
5. Ancient Greece	**10.** Olympic Games

Exercise 6 **Freewriting About a Limited Topic**

Choose one of the limited topics you are considering for your paper. On a separate sheet of paper or your computer, freewrite for several minutes about what you already know about the topic, the questions you have, and any other thoughts or associations that come to mind. Remember, when you freewrite, you don't have to write in complete sentences. Just stay focused on the limited topic, and write down—as fast as you can—all the thoughts, images, questions, and ideas that occur to you. If you are freewriting on a computer, print out what you have written, or save it and back it up.

Exercise 7 Revising Inappropriate Topics

Tell why each topic below is inappropriate for a research paper. Then suggest two alternative but related topics for each. Keep in mind the four requirements for a workable topic. (See pages 10–11.) For example:

Inappropriate. Snowboarding (too general)

Workable. Dangers of snowboarding; comparing and contrasting water–skiing and snowboarding

1. My favorite Mexican foods

2. Space exploration in the year 2050

3. Airport security

4. Native American art

5. Grammy awards

6. Hurricanes

7. William Shakespeare's plays

8. Slang in my grandparents' day

9. Chinese immigration to the United States

_____

_____

10. Solar energy

_____

_____

Exercise 8 **Wording Your Research Questions**

On a separate sheet of paper or your computer, write several research questions for the limited topic that most interests you. These should simply be questions to which you would like to find the answers.

Exercise 9 **Checking Your Progress**

Answer each of the following questions about the work you've done so far.

1. What is the limited topic you have chosen to write about?

_____

_____

2. Are you satisfied with your research questions? Which one(s) appeal to you most?

_____

_____

3. What other topic ideas did you seriously consider? (Write your second and third choices.)

_____

_____

4. How or where did you get the idea for your limited topic?

_____

_____

5. Which approaches to finding and limiting your topic did you try?

_____

_____

6. Which approaches did you think were most useful?

_____

_____

Checklist Review

- ☐ Make sure you understand your assignment.
- ☐ Draw up a project schedule.
- ☐ Choose a workable topic that meets all four requirements for a research paper topic:
    - * You can find enough material on the topic.
    - * The topic interests you, and you think you can make it interest your audience.
    - * The topic is objective, not subjective.
    - * The topic is limited enough to cover adequately in the space available.
- ☐ Word your limited topic as a research question that you are going to investigate.

Locate Sources

ADAM @ HOME © 1998 by UNIVERSAL PRESS SYNDICATE. Reprinted with permission. All rights reserved.

It is now time to locate sources of information you will need for your research paper. In this step you will learn about the many resources available to you and how best to use them. Before starting out on Step 2, however, take a moment to check your progress against the timetable you have chosen as a model (see page 9). Remember, it's important to stay on schedule. Time lost or wasted now will be difficult—maybe impossible—to make up later.

Two Kinds of Sources

As you begin to look for information about your topic, you will explore two kinds of sources. A **primary source** is an original text, document, interview, speech, or letter. It is not someone's comments on or analysis of a text; it is the text itself. A **secondary source** is *not* an original text or document; rather, it is someone's comments on or analysis of a primary source. For example, U.S. census data are a primary source; a study of economic trends based on census data would be a secondary source.

Here are some examples of primary and secondary sources.

PRIMARY SOURCES: Literary works (poems, short stories, novels, essays, plays); documents; autobiographies; letters; interviews; speeches; surveys; tables of statistics

SECONDARY SOURCES: Comments on or analysis (either written or spoken) of an original text or document; biographies

Hint!

Try to include at least one primary source in your paper. Your comments on a primary source will testify to your knowledge about your topic. Primary sources also provide a welcome change from reading about other people's ideas and opinions.

☑ Evaluate the sources that you find.

CHECK THE DATE. You will want accurate, up-to-date information, especially if the topic involves the sciences or social sciences. An article published in 1978 about space stations is seriously out of date, but a 1978 article about William Shakespeare could still be an excellent source. You will have to look at the article to see.

CHECK THE AUTHOR. Is the writer an expert on the topic? You can usually find some information about the writer (educational and career background) on a book's title page or jacket or at the beginning or end of a magazine article. Is there any indication that the writer is biased or unreliable? You need to be especially careful about using information you find on the Internet. (See pages 24–25 on evaluating Internet sources.)

Library/Media Center Resources

Libraries are often called **media centers** these days, and librarians are **media specialists**. That is because most libraries offer videos, audiocassette tapes, CDs, DVDs, computer software, and electronic databases in addition to books, magazines, and newspapers.

☑ Start by exploring library resources.

Remember that you need five or more good sources (or whatever number your teacher has specified), so allow yourself plenty of time to adjust your topic as you turn up new information or run into dead ends. Some sources may be dated; others may be unavailable; some may turn out not to contain any useful information.

USE THE ONLINE CATALOG TO LOCATE BOOKS IN THE LIBRARY. The library's user-friendly computer catalog lets you search for books by author, title, and subject. You might also be able to conduct a **Boolean search**, a title search based on key words. After you enter two or more key words, the computer displays all the book titles containing those key words. If necessary, ask your librarian for help.

When you look up a book in the library's catalog, you will find its **call number**, the series of numbers and letters printed on the book's spine. A call number is like a

Online Research There are a number of ways to get the most out of a Boolean search. In most cases you can pull up titles with variants of key words by using the $ symbol. For example, to find myths about floods in cultures around the world, you might type these key words: *myth$* and *flood$*. The abbreviations *au.* and *ti.*, which stand for "author" and "title," are also useful. For example, if you want to search for books about Willa Cather's *My Ántonia*, you would enter these key words: *cather.au.* and *my antonia.ti.*

road map; it tells you exactly where to find the book you are looking for. Call numbers come from either the **Dewey decimal system** or the **Library of Congress system** for classifying books by their subject. It is not necessary to memorize either system, but you do need to know that the call number of a nonfiction book indicates its general and specific subject and its author's last name. Nonfiction books are shelved according to their call numbers; books of fiction are shelved in a separate section, alphabetically by the author's last name.

USE THE REFERENCE SECTION TO FIND INFORMATION AND SOURCES. The library's reference section contains books and other materials that cannot be checked out. Here are some of the types of resources you can use.

Encyclopedias. Look up your topic in one or more of the standard multivolume encyclopedias, such as *World Book Encyclopedia*, *Encyclopedia Americana*, and *Encyclopaedia Britannica*. Your teacher may not accept encyclopedia articles as sources because they are too broad and general, but they will give you an overview of your topic. Also, at the end of many articles, you will find useful bibliographies— that is, lists of recommended books about the topic. Besides general encyclopedias, you may also find encyclopedias devoted to a single subject, such as the *Grzimek's Animal Life Encyclopedia* series and the *Great Artists of the Western World* series.

Biographical information. If you are tracking down information about a person, the reference section has many multivolume sources (such as *Contemporary Authors* and *Dictionary of Scientific Biography*). Some are published annually (such as *Who's Who in America* and *Current Biography*). You will also find specialized biographical sources (such as *Notable Native Americans*, *Notable Black American Women*, and *Who's Who in the Theatre*).

Atlases. These oversized books contain maps as well as geographical and economic information. There are historical atlases, showing past boundaries, and current atlases, showing nations, cities, and geographic features.

Almanacs. These single-volume books, published each year, are crammed with facts, charts, statistics, and other information.

Dictionaries. A reference section usually has one or more unabridged dictionaries—the oversized ones that contain nearly every word in the English language. There are specialized dictionaries, too, such as dictionaries of slang, sports terms, science, art, and foreign languages.

Quotations. Who said what, and when did he or she say it? If you are trying to track down the source of a familiar phrase or quotation, or if you are looking for a quotation on a specific topic, you will find an assortment of books, such as *Bartlett's Familiar Quotations* and *The Home Book of Quotations*.

Specialized books on all subjects. The reference shelves are filled with many other books that librarians consider useful for research. You will find books about art history, science, math, and many other subjects. You will also find specialized indexes, such as *Book Review Digest*, *The Columbia Granger's Index to Poetry*, *Short Story Index*, *Business Periodicals Index*, and *Humanities Index*.

Research aids. If your topic is a current one, you can jump-start your research by using one of the mini-anthologies that provide articles, background information, and bibliographies about a current topic or issue. Check to see if your library has *Issues and Controversies on File* or *The CQ Researcher*.

LOOK FOR RELEVANT NEWSPAPER AND MAGAZINE ARTICLES. Magazines and newspapers are called **periodicals**. You will find the current ones on library shelves. Back issues are often stored on **microfilm** or **microfiche**. Before you search for magazine or newspaper articles about your topic, find out which periodicals are available in your library. The *Readers' Guide to Periodical Literature* indexes (by subject and author's last name, but not by title) articles in about 200 popular magazines. Ask your librarian for help in using this resource.

Indexes via computer. Your public library may subscribe to one or more indexes of periodicals that you can access via a computer. InfoTrac, for example, lets you search for newspaper and magazine articles by subject and by author. It also gives an **abstract** (brief summary) of many articles and lets you read and print whole articles.

Vertical file. A vertical file is really a file cabinet with folders filed alphabetically by topic, such as Careers, Crime, Hurricanes, Olympic Games, and Peace Corps. The folders contain pamphlets, newspaper articles, government publications, and other materials pertaining to the topic.

Evaluating Internet Sources

Long ago research projects meant working in a library. Now you may be doing much of your research on the Internet—if that's okay with your teacher. Here's an important bit of advice: Don't believe everything you read on the Internet.

☑ Evaluate Internet sources carefully.

Ask yourself these questions about information you discover on the Internet.

* **Who wrote the Web page?** Usually, you can find the name of the writer or organization (and sometimes an e-mail address) somewhere on the home page. How qualified or knowledgeable is the writer? Is the writer an expert or a professional working in the area the Web site discusses?

* **How accurate is the information?** Does the Web page give facts or just the writer's opinions? Verify factual information by locating the same facts in reliable print sources, such as encyclopedias or almanacs.

* **How up-to-date is the information?** Check the date on which the Web site was created and/or last updated.

* **Is the information biased (slanted toward one point of view), or are both sides of an issue presented objectively and fairly?** Bias is difficult to detect unless you know a lot about the topic or issue. Exaggeration, name-calling, and stereotyping are sure clues that the site is biased.

A useful indicator of a Web site's reliability is its **URL** (uniform or universal resource locater), or **address**.

Online **Research** When evaluating an Internet source, look for these **top-level domains** in the address.

* **.gov** indicates that the information is posted by a government agency or group. Agencies such as the U.S. Census Bureau, <http://www.census.gov> and the Department of Labor <http://www.dol.gov> publish detailed statistics that are generally reliable.

* **.edu** is an educational source. A Web site with an *.edu* domain might have been created by someone in a second grade class or someone associated with a college or university. A scholarly project at a university is almost always reliable. For example, <http://xroads.virginia.edu> posts literary texts.

* **.org** is a nonprofit organization. The Web page of a museum should be reliable, but look for bias in an organization sponsoring a cause.

* **.com** is a business. Be wary of information from businesses that are trying to sell you a product. Most major news organizations have reliable sites, such as <http://www.washingtonpost.com> and <http://www.cnn.com>.

* **.net** indicates a variety of organizations that offer Internet services.

Exercise 1 **Match That Source**

For each item in Column A, write the letter of the item in Column B that best describes it.

COLUMN A

_____ 1. *Readers' Guide to Periodical Literature*

_____ 2. atlas

_____ 3. encyclopedia

_____ 4. Internet

_____ 5. Dewey decimal system

_____ 6. *Bartlett's Familiar Quotations*

_____ 7. electronic database

_____ 8. microfilm and microfiche

_____ 9. periodical

_____ 10. library catalog

COLUMN B

a. global network of computer networks

b. book containing maps and geographical information

c. index of articles in magazines and newspapers

d. book (either one or multiple volumes) containing alphabetically arranged articles on a wide range of subjects

e. statistics, facts, information, and articles accessed by computer

f. book of quotations

g. online index of library's books, indexed by subject, title, and author

h. system for classifying and shelving books

i. means of storing back issues of periodicals

j. publication issued at regular intervals (daily, weekly, monthly, etc.), such as a magazine, newspaper, or journal

For each of the research questions listed below, write at least one sentence telling how you would look up information about the topic. (Use a separate sheet of paper or your computer.) What sources would you explore?

1. What are the latest research findings on the effects of dopamine, a chemical that transmits signals in the brain?
2. How do weather forecasters predict the force and track of hurricanes?
3. What is the history of Key West, the southernmost city in the continental United States?
4. What are some of the latest ideas on how to increase voter turnout, such as motor-voter registration (registering to vote when you get a driver's license) and voting by mail?
5. How was the polio epidemic in the United States stopped?
6. What is the story behind Shackleton's 1914–1916 voyage to Antarctica?
7. What is the history of breakthrough motion picture inventions such as sound, color, the blue screen, and animation?
8. What are the major themes of the Mesopotamian epic *Gilgamesh*?
9. What does Picasso's painting *Guernica* represent?
10. What factors led to the extinction of the passenger pigeon?

Exercise 3 Evaluating Internet Sources

For each numbered item, choose the Web site that you would judge most relevant and reliable. Be prepared to explain why you made your choice.

1. For a research paper on the history of lacrosse:
   a. www.lacrosse.com (home page of Great Atlantic Lacrosse Company, featuring lacrosse equipment)
   b. www.lacrosse.org (home page of US Lacrosse, governing body of men's and women's lacrosse in the United States)
   c. www.lacrosseuniversity.com (Web site of Lacrosse University)
   d. www.warriorlacrosse.com (Web site of manufacturer of lacrosse equipment and clothing)

2. For a research paper on Ansel Adams's photographs in Yosemite National Park:
   a. www.nps.gov/yose/nature/articles/adams.htm (Yosemite National Park Web site article about Adams's special relationship with Yosemite)
   b. www.quotationspage.com/quotes/Ansel_Adams (quotations by Ansel Adams)
   c. www.anseladams.com (Web site of Ansel Adams Gallery, which sells photos, posters, books; several pages of biography; bibliography)
   d. www.ncsu.edu/project/farkas/yosemite.html (Adams's photograph of El Capitan and Half Dome with very brief quotation by Adams)

Exercise 4   Getting Started

As you start gathering information for your report, brainstorm a list of library and computer resources that you might explore. (Use a separate sheet of paper or your computer.) Visit the library and start tracking down these sources, adding to your list as you research further. Next to each item on your list, note very briefly those sources that seem useful, those that do not, and why.

Community Resources

☑ Find primary sources by exploring community resources.

Libraries and computers are not the only sources of information. Check out sources in your own community. Who knows a lot about or has had experience related to your topic? Where can you go to find information related to your topic? What questions would you ask an expert? You will create original primary sources as you write letters and conduct interviews and surveys.

WRITE A LETTER TO AN EXPERT. If your topic is the migration pattern of monarch butterflies, you might write to a professor of entomology (the science of studying insects) at a local college or to a local resident who has a large butterfly collection.

Follow these guidelines when you write letters asking for information.

* Find out the person's name, title, and address, and follow the proper form for a business letter.

* Write your letter as soon as you can so that you allow enough time for a reply. (The problem with gathering information by writing letters is that you have no control over how quickly you will receive a reply.)

* Be polite, and ask specific questions that show you already have some knowledge of your topic.

* If you receive a reply, write a short note thanking the person for the information you've received.

Exercise 5   Writing a Letter

Write a letter to someone who might provide you with information on the topic you have chosen for your report. Find the name of the person, the person's complete address (including the ZIP code), and write the letter. You do not have to restrict yourself to people in your community; you can write to anyone who might have personal knowledge about your topic. Be sure to follow the proper form for a business letter. As a model you might use the letter shown on page 28.

13001 Marigold Lane
Silver Spring, MD 20906
November 22, 2004

Ms. Selma Owens, Director of Communications
Maryland Youth Lacrosse League
8010 Loch Raven Boulevard
Towson, MD 21285

Dear Ms. Owens:

I am a 9th grade student at John F. Kennedy High School. I am writing a research paper on lacrosse and am especially interested in Youth Lacrosse. Can you please tell me about the history of Youth Lacrosse in the United States?

I would also like to know what a school has to do in order to start a lacrosse team. And if you have any publications that describe the rules and regulations of Youth Lacrosse, I would really appreciate your sending this information to me.

Thank you for your help. I look forward to hearing from you.

Sincerely,

Benjamin Spragg

Benjamin Spragg

CONDUCT AN INTERVIEW IN PERSON OR ON THE TELEPHONE. Instead of writing letters to ask questions, you might call or write someone knowledgeable about your topic to arrange for an interview. Follow these important steps.

* Before you get started, make sure that you have your teacher's permission for the interview.
* Either by letter or phone, explain to the interviewee who you are, what you are writing about, and why you think he or she might be helpful.

* Ask for a limited amount of time, perhaps 30 minutes, and set a definite day and time for the interview.

* Before the interview, prepare five to ten clearly worded questions that will yield specific information and guide the interview. Keep in mind that a prepared question may bring a reply that leads to other questions and answers. It is important to remain flexible enough to pursue unexpected leads.

* Appear (or call) promptly for the interview. Be polite and take notes. If you are going to record the interview, ask for permission in advance.

* Ask for permission to use direct quotes from the interview in your paper.

* Don't overstay your welcome. Thank the person for his or her time, and send a follow-up letter of thanks.

Exercise 6 — Preparing for an Interview

Draft five questions you would ask each of the following persons in an interview on the topic given. Phrase your questions in a way that will encourage the person interviewed to respond with specific details. You might work with a partner to test your questions.

1. A famous sports figure (name him or her) on how to prepare for a career in his or her field

   Name of person: _____

   _____

   _____

   _____

   _____

   _____

2. A local government official on juvenile crime (or any other serious issue) in your community

   Name of person: _____

   _____

   _____

   _____

   _____

   _____

3. Your school principal (or a school board member or the superintendent of schools) on an education issue (curriculum, safety, budget, class size, educational reform, vocational education, dropouts, etc.)

Name of person: _____

_____

_____

_____

_____

_____

VISIT A LOCAL MUSEUM OR GOVERNMENT OFFICE. You might sit in on a city council meeting or visit a local recycling plant. Is there a museum related to your topic nearby? You might find there exactly the information you need for your report. Check with the librarian or curator at the museum for help in tracking down the information you need. If you visit a government office, request publications or other information from a receptionist, who will steer you to the proper person.

Exercise 7   Focusing on Your Community

On a separate sheet of paper or your computer, write a few sentences for each of the research questions below, telling where and how you would find information in your community. List specific names and addresses if possible.

1. What organized after-school athletic programs are available for elementary school boys and girls in your community?

2. What is your community doing or planning to do about recycling? How successful have recycling projects been during the last three years?

3. What specific resources does the community provide for senior citizens? What needs are not being met? How might the community meet these needs?

4. What is the procedure for deciding how local taxes are spent? What were last year's expenditures, and what is the proposed budget for the coming year?

5. What local organizations are available for people interested in the arts? Are there music groups, theater groups, book groups?

6. Who are the current members of the local school board, and how are they elected? How are changes in school policy decided?

7. How many law enforcement officers are there in your community? What training do they undergo before they join the force?

8. Who are your elected representatives in the state legislature? Who are your elected representatives in Congress? How can you reach each of them?

9. What are the most recent statistics on crime in your community? Are serious crimes on the rise, or are they declining?

10. What percentage of the ninth grade class in your school goes on to graduate from high school? What percentage of the high school graduates go on to college?

CONDUCT A SURVEY. When you conduct a survey, you have a chance to ask people everything you want to know about your topic. First, you will have to figure out a useful **sampling**, the group of people you will ask to complete your questionnaire. Then you will have to write clearly worded questions designed to elicit the information you are looking for. Instead of providing blank lines and asking people to write in their own answers to your questions, give them a choice of responses. This way it is easier to tally the results.

Here is an example of a survey question and a choice of responses.

EXAMPLE

```
How many hours of television do you watch on an average
weekday during the school year? (Include both daytime and
evening viewing.)
    ☐ none          ☐ less than 1      ☐ 1-2 hours
    ☐ 2-3 hours     ☐ 3-5 hours        ☐ 6 or more hours
```

Creating a survey or questionnaire takes careful planning. Consider all the following questions:

✱ Who will be your sampling, and how many people will you survey? (The larger and more random the sample, the more accurate or representative your information will be. For example, instead of surveying just your close friends, you will get a more random sampling by surveying every other person in three or four homerooms at different grade levels.)

✱ How can you ensure that you will get enough responses?

✱ Whose permission will you need to distribute your questionnaire?

✱ What specific information do you want to find?

✱ Are your questions clearly worded? (You might try out your survey on several friends.)

✱ Are the responses designed so that they can be tallied easily?

✱ What conclusions can you make based on the results of your survey?

Exercise 8   **Conducting a Survey**

Pretend that as part of your research paper on the TV-watching habits of students, you are going to conduct a survey. On a separate sheet of paper or your computer, draft at least six questions with responses that can be tallied easily. Compare your questions with those of your classmates. You might create a class questionnaire and distribute it to other English classes. Tally the results, and decide what you can conclude from the survey.

Exercise 9 Getting Started

On a separate sheet of paper or your computer, name one primary source that you plan to explore for your research paper: a letter, an interview, a visit , a survey. Detail the steps you will use, and compose whatever needs to be written.

a. **Letter.** If you are writing a letter asking for information, find out the name, title, and address of a person who might provide the information. Draft the letter, revise it, and send it. Report to a classmate or classmates on the reply you receive.

b. **Interview.** Find out the name of a person you might interview. Draft ten questions you would ask that person. (Be sure to word your questions so that you get more than a *yes* or *no* answer.) Choose your best questions (at least six), and call or write to arrange for an interview. Be sure your teacher approves your interview plans.

c. **Visit.** Determine if there is a local museum or government office that might have information that you need on your topic. Find out the location and hours when you can visit. Plan your visit, and write down the information you gather.

d. **Survey.** Think of a survey that might help you gather useful information for your report. Who would take the survey? Draft a questionnaire (at least seven or eight questions with responses), revise it, and distribute it to your sample. Tally your results, and decide what conclusions you can draw.

Bibliography Cards: Keeping Track of Sources

☑ **Record complete information for every source you think you will use.**

For every source you consult, you will make a bibliography card on a 3" x 5" or 4" x 6" index card. On each card, you will record the author, title, and publishing information. You may also find it helpful to add your own note or comment about the source. You will use these bibliography cards to create your "Works Cited" page, which lists all the sources used in the paper. For this reason it is important to assign each card a source number (see the upper right-hand corner of each sample card shown on page 33). The source number will help you save time and keep track of where your notes come from.

Book

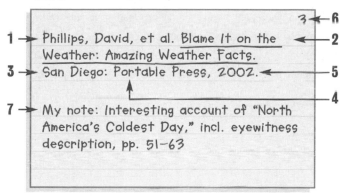

1 → Phillips, David, et al. Blame It on the ← 2
Weather: Amazing Weather Facts.
3 → San Diego: Portable Press, 2002. ← 5

4

7 → My note: Interesting account of "North
America's Coldest Day," incl. eyewitness
description, pp. 51–63

Newspaper or Magazine Article

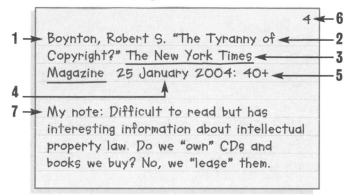

1 → Boynton, Robert S. "The Tyranny of ← 2
Copyright?" The New York Times ← 3
Magazine   25 January 2004: 40+ ← 5
4
7 → My note: Difficult to read but has
interesting information about intellectual
property law. Do we "own" CDs and
books we buy? No, we "lease" them.

1 Author(s), if given
2 Article's title, enclosed
   in quotation marks
3 Newspaper's or maga-
   zine's title, underlined
4 Date of publication
5 Page(s) on which article
   appears
6 Researcher's source
   number
7 Researcher's comment

☑ Write each bibliography entry according to the style your teacher requires.

You will follow the exact same style when you write the entries for your Works Cited list, so getting the entries right on the bibliography source cards will save you a lot of time later. In the sample bibliography cards above and the entries on pages 34–38, pay special attention to three things:

* the information that is given

* the order in which the information is given

* the punctuation of each item

The entries in this book follow the **MLA (Modern Language Association)** style for documenting sources, which is the style most often required by high school and college teachers. (For the APA style, see Appendix C.) Whatever style of documentation your teacher requires, be sure to follow it exactly.

The following pages show examples of the MLA style for documenting sources. Unless your teacher directs you to use a different style, this is the style you will use to prepare your Works Cited list or **bibliography**. Each example shows the necessary information, the order in which it is given, and the proper punctuation. In every entry in a Works Cited list, turnover lines are indented five spaces.

MLA Style of Documenting Sources

☑ Books

BOOK BY A SINGLE AUTHOR

Tan, Amy. The Opposite of Fate: A Book of Musings. New York: Putnam's, 2003.

TWO OR MORE BOOKS BY THE SAME AUTHOR

After the first mention of an author's name, use three hyphens followed by a period to indicate "same author as above."

Austen, Jane. Northanger Abbey. Ed. Anne Henry Ehrenpreis. London: Penguin, 1985.

---. Persuasion. Ed. D. W. Harding. London: Penguin, 1985.

BOOK BY TWO AUTHORS

Cosby, Camille O., and Renee Poussaint. A Wealth of Wisdom: Legendary African American Elders Speak. New York: Atria, 2004.

BOOK BY THREE OR MORE AUTHORS

You may list all the authors in the order in which they are listed on the title page, or you may list only the first author followed by the abbreviation *et al.* ("and others"). Either style is acceptable. Find out which one your teacher prefers.

Elias, Maurice J., Steven E. Tobias, and Brian S. Friedlander. Raising Emotionally Intelligent Teenagers. New York: Harmony, 2000.

Greenough, Sarah, et al. On the Art of Fixing a Shadow: One Hundred and Fifty Years of Photography. Washington, DC: National Gallery of Art, 1989.

BOOK BY A SINGLE EDITOR

Kennedy, Caroline, ed. A Patriot's Handbook: Songs, Poems, Stories, and Speeches Celebrating the Land We Love. New York: Hyperion, 2003.

BOOK BY SINGLE AUTHOR WITH EDITORS AND TRANSLATOR

Frank, Anne. The Diary of a Young Girl: The Definitive Edition. Ed. Otto H. Frank and Mirjam Pressler. Trans. Susan Massotty. New York: Doubleday, 1995.

BOOK BY TWO EDITORS

Goldhammer, Arthur, and Christine Klapish-Zuber, eds. <u>A History of Women in the West, Vol. 2: Silences of the Middle Ages</u>. Cambridge, MA: Belknap, 1994.

BOOK BY THREE OR MORE EDITORS

Appiah, Kwame Anthony, et al., eds. <u>The Dictionary of Global Culture</u>. New York: Knopf, 1996.

Perkins, George, Barbara Perkins, and Phillip Leininger, eds. <u>Benét's Reader's Encyclopedia of American Literature</u>. New York: Harper, 1991.

BOOK WITH NO AUTHOR CITED

<u>The Baseball Encyclopedia</u>. 8th ed. New York: Macmillan, 1990.

BOOK THAT IS PART OF A SERIES

Soumerai, Eva Nussbaum, and Carol D. Schulz. <u>A Voice from the Holocaust</u>. Voices of Twentieth-Century Conflict Ser. Westport, CT: Greenwood, 2003.

MULTIVOLUME WORK

Hunter, Jeffrey W., et al., eds. <u>Contemporary Literary Criticism</u>. Vol. 148. Farmington Hills, MI: Gale, 2002.

EDITION

Lincoln, C. Eric. <u>The Black Muslims in America</u>. 3rd ed. Trenton, NJ: Africa World, 1994.

TRANSLATION

Appelfeld, Aharon. <u>To the Land of the Cattails</u>. Trans. Jeffrey M. Green. New York: Grove, 1994.

GOVERNMENT PUBLICATION

United States. U.S. General Accounting Office. <u>Student Testing: Current Extent and Expenditures, with Cost Estimates for a National Examination</u>. Washington, DC: GAO, 1993.

PAMPHLET

Stevenson, George B. <u>Trees of Everglades National Park and the Florida Keys</u>. 2nd ed. Miami: Banyon, 1969.

☑ Parts of Books

STORY, ESSAY, POEM, OR PLAY IN A BOOK BY A SINGLE AUTHOR

Erdrich, Louise. "Indian Boarding School: The Runaways." <u>Original Fire: Selected and New Poems</u>. New York: Harper, 2003.

STORY, ESSAY, POEM, OR PLAY IN AN ANTHOLOGY

Hurston, Zora Neal. "Drenched in Light." <u>The Portable Harlem Renaissance Reader</u>. Ed. David Levering Lewis. New York: Viking, 1994. 691–98.

García Márquez, Gabriel. "A Very Old Man with Enormous Wings." Trans. Gregory Rabassa. <u>Collected Stories</u>. New York: Harper, 1984. 203–10.

INTRODUCTION, FOREWORD, OR PREFACE
By the author of the work

Porter, Katherine Anne. "Go Little Book . . ." Preface. The Collected Stories of
    Katherine Anne Porter. New York: Harcourt, 1965. v–vi.

By someone other than the author of a work

Baldwin, James. "Sweet Lorraine." Introduction. To Be Young, Gifted and Black. By
    Lorraine Hansberry, adapted by Robert Nemiroff. Englewood Cliffs, NJ:
    Prentice, 1969. ix–xii.

ARTICLE IN AN ENCYCLOPEDIA OR OTHER REFERENCE BOOK
Unsigned

For a familiar reference work, you do not have to cite the city and publisher.
Articles from less familiar reference books should have full publishing information
(place of publication and publisher).

"Islamic Art and Architecture." The Columbia Encyclopedia. 6th ed. 2001.

"Dominican Republic." Statesman's Year-Book, 1995–96. 132nd ed. Ed. Brian
    Hunter. New York: St. Martin's, 1995. 492–96.

Signed

Wiggins, David K. "Jesse Owens." The Oxford Companion to United States History.
    New York: Oxford, 2001.

☑ Magazine and Newspaper Articles
MAGAZINE ARTICLE

Notice how the date (day of month followed by abbreviated month) and page numbers
are cited. Do not cite volume or issue numbers. A plus sign (+) indicates that the
article begins on that page and is continued on the following pages, which are not
consecutive.

King, Peter. "NFL Playoffs: Coming Through." Sports Illustrated 26 Jan. 2004: 42–47.

Tyson, Neil deGrasse. "Great Masses from Little Ripples Grew." Natural History Feb.
    2004: 18+.

NEWSPAPER ARTICLE

Battista, Judy. "Patriots Take 2nd Super Bowl in Last 3 Years." New York Times 2
    Feb. 2004, southern ed., sec. 1: 1.

NEWSPAPER EDITORIAL

"The Defense Speaks." Editorial. Washington Post 18 Jan. 2004: B6.

NEWSPAPER COLUMN

Lipsyte, Robert. "Cheating Wends Way from Youth Sports to Business." USA Today
    10 Dec. 2003, late ed., sec. A: 23.

LETTER TO THE EDITOR

Impola, Richard A. Letter. New York Times 18 Mar. 2004, late ed., sec. A: 32.

☑ Electronic Sources

In addition to electronic publication information, you must include the date you accessed the site.

ONLINE MAGAZINE ARTICLE

Landsburg, Steven E. "Grade Expectations." Slate 12 Aug. 1999. 12 Jan. 2000
        <http://slate.msn.com/id/33044>.

ONLINE NEWSPAPER ARTICLE

Associated Press. "Freeing Willy, in Real Life." New York Times on the Web 8 Sept.
        1999. 22 Dec. 1999 <http://search.nytimes.com/>.

ONLINE REFERENCE WORK

Tufts, Eleanor. "Cassatt, Mary." Grolier Multimedia Encyclopedia. 2004. Scholastic.
        19 Sept. 2004 <http://gme.grolier.com>.

SCHOLARLY PROJECT

The Avalon Project. 1996–2003. Yale U. Law School 2 June 2003
        <http://www.yale.edu/lawweb/avalon/diplomacy/forrel/cuba/cubamenu.htm>.

PROFESSIONAL WEB SITE

Victorian Women Writers Project. Ed. Perry Willett. Dec. 2000. Indiana U. 3 Feb.
        2003 <http://www.indiana.edu/~letrs/vwwp/>.

POSTING TO A NEWSGROUP OR FORUM

Sussman, Mick. "'The Great Gatsby' by F. Scott Fitzgerald." Online posting. 1 Apr.
        2002. 2003 Reading Group Archive. 18 Mar. 2004
        <http://forums.nytimes.com/top/opinion/readersopinions/forums/books/2003
        readinggrouparchive/thegreatgatsbybyfscottfitzgerald/index.html>.

E-MAIL

Hadley, Karen. "Re: Chocolate." E-mail to the author. 27 July 2004.

CD-ROM ENCYCLOPEDIA ARTICLE

"Antarctica." Complete Reference Collection. CD-ROM. The Learning Company, 1997.

☑ Other Sources

TELEVISION OR RADIO PROGRAM

Evening News with Peter Jennings. ABC. WPLG, Miami. 12 Feb. 2004.

SOUND RECORDING (TAPE, CD, LP)

Tolkien, J. R. R. The Fellowship of the Ring. The Lord of the Rings, Book One.
        Narrated by Rob Inglis. 12 audiocassettes. Recorded Books, 2001.

FILM OR VIDEO RECORDING

Fooling with Words: A Bill Moyers Special. Dir. Catherine Tatqe. Films for the Humani. 1999.

The Grapes of Wrath. Dir. John Ford. With John Carradine, Jane Darwell, and Henry Fonda. Writ. Nunnally Johnson. Twentieth Century-Fox, 1940.

PERFORMANCE (CONCERT, PLAY, OPERA, BALLET)

To Be Young, Gifted and Black. By Lorraine Hansberry. Dir. Gene Frankel. With Barbara Baxley, Rita Gardner, Janet League, Cicely Tyson, John Beal, Gertrude Jeanette, Stephen Strimpell, Andre Womble. Cherry Lane Theatre, New York. 2 Jan. 1969.

WORK OF ART

Hopper, Edward. Office in a Small City. Metropolitan Museum of Art, New York.

INTERVIEW
Published interview

Drossos, George. Interview. Division Street America. By Studs Terkel. New York: Pantheon, 1967. 93–96.

Unpublished interview

Santiago, Fabiola. Personal interview. 28 Feb. 2004.

LETTER
Published letter

Crane, Stephen. "To Joseph Conrad." 17 Mar. 1898. Letter 228 in Stephen Crane: Letters. Ed. R. W. Stallman and Lillian Gilkes. New York: New York UP, 1960. 176–77.

Unpublished letter

Angelou, Maya. Letter to the author. 6 Mar. 2003.

MAP OR CHART

Texas. Map. Chicago: Rand, 2000.

CARTOON

Stavro/Lebanon. Cartoon. Miami Herald 2 Feb. 2004: 18A.

LECTURE, SPEECH, OR ADDRESS

Faulkner, William. Nobel Prize speech. City Hall, Stockholm, Sweden. 10 Dec. 1950.

Kennedy, John F. Inaugural address. Washington, DC. 20 Jan. 1961.

Exercise 10 — Preparing Bibliography Source Card Entries

Write a bibliography source card entry for each of the following items, using the MLA style shown on the preceding pages. Be sure to give the information in the proper order and use the correct punctuation.

1. Scott [first name] Adams is the author of a book of cartoons titled Dilbert and the Way of the Weasel. It was published in 2002. The publisher is HarperBusiness, which is located in New York.

2. Peter James and Nick Thorpe are the two editors of a book called *Ancient Inventions*. Their publisher is Ballantine Books in New York. The book appeared in 1999.

3. Jay Hyams is the translator and Giovanni [first name] Pinna is the author of a book about fossils. Its title is *The Illustrated Encyclopedia of Fossils*. It was published in 1990 by Facts on File in New York.

4. The author of a biography called *W. B. Yeats: A Life* is R. F. Foster. The biography is subtitled *Vol. II: The Arch-Poet (1915–1939)*. The book is published by Oxford University Press, which is located in Oxford, UK. It was published in 2003.

Exercise 11 — What Is Wrong with These Bibliography Source Card Entries?

Each of the following bibliography source card entries contains at least one error; some contain many errors. Rewrite each entry, following exactly the MLA style as described on pages 34–38. Check carefully the punctuation, the information included, and the order in which the information is given.

1. Ralph Hickok. A Who's Who of Sports Champions. Houghton Mifflin, New York, 1995.

_____

_____

_____

2. Editor, Jeff Silverman. Text by Lardner, Ring. Lardner on Baseball. 2002, Lyons Press in Guilford, CT.

_____

_____

_____

3. Allende, Isabel. Paula. Translated by Margaret Sayers Peden. 1994, HarperCollins: New York.

_____

_____

_____

4. Isaac Victor Kerlow. <u>The Art of 3D: Computer Animation and Effects, Third edition</u>. Hoboken, NJ, John Wiley & Sons. 2004. 3rd edition.

_____

_____

_____

5. Glanz, James, "Uut and Uup Add Their Atomic Mass to Periodic Table" in New York Times, a newspaper, February 1, 2004, page 1 southern edition, section YT.

_____

_____

_____

6. Kennedy, Joseph. "The Wild Man of Samoa." <u>Natural History</u>, a magazine. Feb. 2004. Pages 22–25, 66.

_____

_____

_____

Exercise 12 Exploring Sources

On a separate sheet of paper or your computer, list every source that you explore as you do research for your paper. Follow exactly the MLA style for documenting sources, as shown on pages 34–38. Write a bibliography card for each source that you think will be useful.

Exercise 13 Checking Your Progress

Answer each of the following questions about the work you've done so far.

1. Of the sources that you explored, which ones did you choose as the most relevant and reliable? Where did you find each of these sources?

_____

_____

2. How many bibliography source cards have you made so far? How many sources does your teacher require?

_____

_____

3. What community resources have you explored?

_____

_____

4. How did you judge which Internet sources are most reliable?

_____

_____

5. If you need to find more sources, where will you look?

_____

_____

Checklist Review

☐ Evaluate the sources that you find to make sure they are relevant and reliable. Be especially careful to evaluate Internet sources.

☐ Start by exploring library resources.
   * Use the online catalog to locate books.
   * Use the reference section to find information and sources.
   * Look for relevant newspaper and magazine articles.

☐ Find primary sources by exploring community resources.
   * Write a letter to an expert.
   * Conduct an interview in person or on the telephone.
   * Visit a local museum or government office.
   * Conduct a survey.

☐ Record complete information for every source you think you will use.
☐ Write each bibliography entry according to the style your teacher requires.

Take Notes

BIG NATE reprinted by permission of Newspaper Enterprise Association, Inc.

Now that you have tracked down your sources, you are about to start the task of gathering information for your research paper. Note-taking is a crucial step on the way to your finished paper. If you do a good job taking notes, all the rest of the steps in completing your research paper will be a lot easier. But if you are careless—if, for example, you do not take care to record and credit your sources fully and accurately—you will make more work for yourself later on.

Working Outline

☑ Before you start taking notes, make a working outline.

Stop to make a plan, a road map to see where you are headed. Like all outlines, a working outline lists main topics and subtopics in some kind of logical order, but a working outline is informal and definitely not final. (You will make your final outline later.) Its purpose is to guide your research and note-taking. The following questions will help you plan your working outline.

- ✱ What are my research questions, the questions I want to find the answers to?
- ✱ What are the most important ideas I want to cover in my paper?
- ✱ What background information will readers need to have?
- ✱ What are the main parts, or sections, of my paper, and how do they relate to one another?
- ✱ How might I best organize the information?
- ✱ What conclusion(s) do I expect to draw?

You will probably revise your working outline several times as you take notes and think about your paper. You may decide to drop, add, change, or rearrange topics and subtopics as you discover, or are unable to find, the information that you are looking for.

Here is an example of a working outline for a paper about lacrosse.

EXAMPLE

                    Lacrosse: Yesterday and Today
  I. History of lacrosse
     A. Developed by Native Americans
        1. A violent game called "baggataway"
        2. Used to train warriors
     B. Adopted by French settlers in Canada
        1. Called lacrosse
        2. 1856—Montreal Lacrosse Club
        3. 1860—rules standardized
 II. How the game is played
     A. Teams
     B. Rules
     C. Equipment
III. Lacrosse today
     A. For both women and men
     B. In high schools
     C. In colleges
     D. International lacrosse

Exercise 1 — **Making a Working Outline for Your Paper**

On a separate sheet of paper or your computer, write a working outline for your research paper. Think about the main ideas you want to cover and how best to arrange them. Remember that you will probably revise this working outline as you continue to research and take notes.

☑ Skim your sources to locate information for your paper.

Skimming is the very fast type of reading you use when you search for specific information or for a particular kind of information.

Here's how to skim for information if your source is a book:

* Turn to the index (if there is one) at the back of the book or to the table of contents at the front. Look for headings related to your topic and research questions.

* When you find a heading that seems useful, turn to the page(s) listed and skim to see if that page or section of the book has the information you want.

✱ Force your eyes to move very quickly until you find the information you want or decide that it is not there.

To skim a newspaper, magazine, or encyclopedia article, read each subhead and quickly glance at the paragraphs, paying special attention to the first and last sentences of each.

Hint!

Not every source you explore will have useful information. Don't waste time reading a source slowly or taking notes once you have decided the source isn't useful.

Exercise 2 — Practice Skimming to Locate Information

Force yourself to read at top speed as you look for specific information. Use a daily newspaper to do this exercise.

1. If you watch television tonight at 8 P.M., what program will you choose to watch? What channel is it on? What program is playing tonight on your local public television channel at 8:00?

_____

_____

2. What is the main subject of each of the editorials on the editorial page?

_____

_____

3. In one sentence, summarize the most important story in today's newspaper. (A newspaper's most important story is usually in the upper-right-hand column of the front page of the first section.)

_____

_____

4. Write the headline and the name of the author of a story that appears in the sports section. Then summarize the story in one sentence.

_____

_____

_____

Exercise 3 — Skimming One of Your Sources

Skim one of the sources you have listed in Step 2, Exercise 12, to see if you can find information that is directly related to your topic. Write down the information as it is listed in the source and the page number(s) on which the information is located. Circle all the page numbers that contain information you think will be useful enough for you to take notes. (NOTE: When you are checking the rest of your sources, you won't write this information down or circle page numbers. You will start taking notes on note cards as soon as you locate useful information.)

1. Title and author of source

_____

_____

2. Information related to (name of topic)

_____

3. Page number(s) where information is located

_____

_____

Avoiding Plagiarism

In your finished paper, you must not copy the words or ideas of another writer without giving that writer credit. You cannot even come _close_ to copying. If you do, you are guilty of **plagiarism**, stealing another person's words and/or ideas and passing them off as your own. Plagiarism, which comes from a Latin word meaning "kidnapper," is totally unacceptable. It is a very serious academic offense and carries very serious consequences. Don't even _think_ about plagiarizing. You will almost certainly get a failing grade on your paper and perhaps even in the course.

There are basically two kinds of plagiarism: **intentional** and **accidental**. In intentional plagiarism, students copy word for word large chunks of material from published or online sources. Or they may "borrow" another student's entire research paper (one used in a previous year) and pass it off as their own. They may even buy a research paper offered for sale on the Internet.

Students are always amazed when they are caught, surprised that their teachers can so easily detect this type of plagiarism. But they shouldn't be surprised. Teachers have a good idea of the writing style and capabilities of each of their students, and they are suspicious whenever phrases, sentences, paragraphs, or sometimes even a whole paper does not "sound" like a particular student's work.

Accidental plagiarism occurs when you forget that you are quoting a source and don't give proper credit. To avoid this kind of plagiarism, it's essential that when you take notes, you do something to ensure that you will be able to distinguish your own words and thoughts from those of a writer. (For two foolproof techniques, see guidelines 5 and 6 on page 47.) It's usually a long time between the time you take notes and the time you begin drafting your paper, so make sure that your note cards are crystal clear about who said what.

GIVING CREDIT. A **paraphrase** is a restatement of a writer's ideas in your own words. Suppose you are paraphrasing a writer's ideas from one of your sources. Even though you are not copying the writer's exact words, you are using the writer's ideas. Unless you give credit to the original writer, you are plagiarizing.

It is not enough simply to mention in passing that information you are presenting in your paper is paraphrased from the work of another author. The acknowledgment must be formal: a parenthetical reference to the original source, which is listed on the Works Cited page. (Rules and guidelines for documenting sources are covered in Step 7.) In the example that follows, note that the writer not only refers to the book and the author being paraphrased (*Cosmos* by Carl Sagan) but also cites the page number where the original material is located in that book. (Since the book title is given in the passage, the writer only needs to cite the page.) Had the writer failed to credit the original author in this fashion, he or she would be guilty of plagiarism.

In <u>Cosmos</u>, based on his thirteen-part television series, Carl Sagan describes the extraordinary songs of whales and dolphins. Because sight and smell are not much use in cloudy ocean waters, Sagan explains, these underwater mammals communicate by means of sound. Humpback whales have extraordinary memories, and scientists have recorded exact repetitions of whale songs that last anywhere from 15 minutes to an hour. Sometimes groups of whales sing in unison. They are clearly communicating, but no one has figured out what the songs mean (271).

Taking Notes on Note Cards

When you find information that you think will be useful for your paper, it's time to adjust your reading speed. Slow down from skimming speed to the pace you use when you are trying to understand information. If you are like most readers, that means you will read every sentence, not skipping any words, and concentrate on the meaning of what you are reading. You still will not take notes on everything you find, just on information that you think might be useful for your paper.

☑ Follow these eight guidelines for taking notes.

1. Use 3" x 5" cards or 4" x 6" cards. (Or you can cut pieces of paper to either of these sizes.)

2. Write the source number in the upper-right-hand corner of the card. On each card take notes from only one source.

3. Write on only one side of each card, and write about only one main idea. (You will then be able to arrange and rearrange your note cards easily according to their main ideas.)

4. Write a heading—a key word or phrase—at the top of the note card and under-line it. The heading indicates the main idea discussed on the note card. Usually, the heading is one of the topics or subtopics in your working outline.

5. Make a conscious effort to use your own words when you take notes. It may help to close the book and explain to yourself what the author has written, then write that explanation on your note card. You do not need to write in complete sentences. Use abbreviations and symbols.

6. Enclose direct quotations in large quotation marks. Make sure you have quoted word for word, *exactly* as the author wrote it. If you wish to leave out any material (a sentence or phrase or even a single word) from the quoted passage, you must show that you have done so by inserting ellipses at the appropriate point. (For more information on ellipses and other changes to quoted material, see Step 6.)

7. At the bottom of each note card, write the page number(s) where you found the information.

8. Before you go on to a new note card, double-check to see that you have written the source number and page numbers. If you haven't done this, your note card will be useless because you will not be able to find and document the source of your information again.

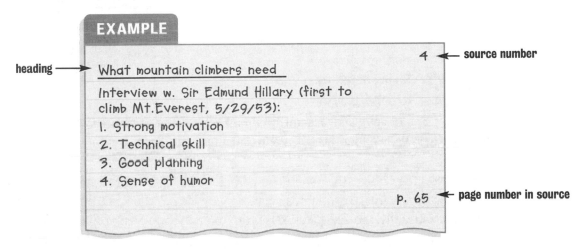

EXAMPLE

heading → What mountain climbers need
Interview w. Sir Edmund Hillary (first to climb Mt.Everest, 5/29/53):
1. Strong motivation
2. Technical skill
3. Good planning
4. Sense of humor

4 ← source number

p. 65 ← page number in source

E-writing If you have the use of a laptop, you can take it with you to the library (or any other place you visit to find information) and take notes directly on the computer. Or you can keyboard your notes at school or at home. Save your notes in a separate file or document, and be sure to print out a hard copy—just in case something happens to the file or to the computer.

You can make sorting through your notes (the first job in Step 4) a lot easier if you group together all the notes with the same heading (key word or phrase at the top of the note card). Here's how to do it: Write your heading, and then hit the Search or Find command in the Edit menu. Search for that same heading elsewhere in your notes. If you find another note with the same heading, cut and paste it to the same place. Then, when you print your notes, you will have them neatly grouped by heading.

Three Kinds of Notes

Your notes will probably contain a mixture of direct quotations, paraphrases, and summaries.

DIRECT QUOTATIONS. Sometimes you will find a writer's wording so vivid or effective that you decide you might want to quote it in your paper. On your note card, copy the quote exactly, word for word, just as the writer wrote it, and enclose the quoted material in large quotation marks. (Later on, when you review your notes, the jumbo quotes will alert you immediately that the wording isn't yours.)

EXAMPLE

I

The Great Gatsby
F. Scott Fitzgerald letter to Maxwell
Perkins (editor) about plans for 3rd novel:
"I want to write something new—something
extraordinary and beautiful and simple +
intricately patterned."

p. 112

Hint!

In your finished paper, keep direct quotations brief, and use them sparingly. Think of sprinkling a handful or two of direct quotations throughout your paper. No more than one-fifth of your total paper should be direct quotations.

 Exercise 4 — **Taking Notes for a Direct Quotation**

Look through one of your sources until you find a sentence or phrase you might quote directly in your paper. Fill out a note card for that direct quotation.

PARAPHRASING. Remember that when you paraphrase a text, you restate the writer's ideas in your own words. A paraphrase covers every idea in the same order as in the original but is usually shorter. Paraphrases are most useful when you are writing about a short literary text, such as a poem. Here is a paraphrase of Robert Frost's "The Road Not Taken."

> The speaker in the poem remembers a time when he was walking in the autumn woods and came to a place where he had to choose between two roads. He stood there a long time, feeling sad that he could not travel both. After peering down one road as far as he could see, he chose the other, grassier one. Both roads were worn about the same and were covered with fresh leaves. He told himself he would go down the other road someday but didn't really think he would ever be back. He says that he will be telling about this choice many years in the future. His taking the less-traveled road was an important turning point in his life.

Exercise 5   Paraphrasing

Choose an important paragraph from one of your sources. On a separate sheet of paper or your computer, write a paraphrase of it. With a partner, compare your paraphrase with the original text. Have you included all the writer's ideas in the same order as in the original? Have you used *your own* words? Have you credited the original source?

SUMMARIZING. When you summarize something, you restate the main ideas in your own words. A summary does not give all the details, only the most important ones. Here, for example, are several paragraphs about utopias, followed by a brief summary.

ORIGINAL TEXT

Do you think you would like to live in a utopia? The word *utopia* is a made-up word that means, literally, "not a place." Sir Thomas More made up the word from the ancient Greek *ou-* (not) and *topos* (a place). More, a prominent English author and statesman, described the island of Utopia in a political essay in 1516. In More's *Utopia*, men and women are equally educated (unheard of at the time), and all religions are tolerated. More's Utopia is an ideal society in which every person thrives and injustice, poverty, and misery no longer exist. More's *Utopia*, published in Latin, was an immediate success. Unfortunately for More, his conflict with King Henry VIII over Henry's desire to break from the Roman Catholic church led to More's beheading in 1535.

Gradually, the words *utopia* and *utopian* have come to refer to any ideal society. Since More's day, others have written about such societies, most notably Samuel Butler in *Erewhon* (1872), an anagram of the word *nowhere*, and Edward Bellamy in *Looking Backward* (1888). B. F. Skinner's *Walden Two* (1961) depicts an ideal community based on the writer's behavioral psychology theories. All these utopian works criticize contemporary society and propose remedies for society's ills. Satires of utopian societies abound, including Jonathan Swift's *Gulliver's Travels* (1726), Aldous Huxley's *Brave New World* (1932), and George Orwell's *1984* (1949). The latter two portray *dystopias*, societies in which something is vastly wrong.

SUMMARY

> The word "utopia" comes from the ideal society Sir Thomas More described in a political essay in 1516. More called his island Utopia, from the Greek for "not a place." Utopian literature does two things: criticizes what is wrong with the writer's society and suggests ways to fix society's injustices and other problems. Other utopian novels include Bellamy's <u>Looking Backward</u>, Butler's <u>Erewhon</u>, and Skinner's <u>Walden Two</u>. Swift's <u>Gulliver's Travels</u>, Huxley's <u>Brave New World</u>, and Orwell's <u>1984</u> are satires of utopias.

Keep in mind that when you are taking notes, you do not have to use complete sentences. Words, phrases, and fragments are fine—just as long as you can understand later what you have written on your note card and you make sure to avoid plagiarism.

EXAMPLE

<u>Meaning of utopia</u>   2

Utopia (Gr., "not a place"). Made up by Sir Thomas More, name of island & ideal society in his essay <u>Utopia</u> (1516). Utopia & utopian = any ideal society

                                                              p. 426

Hint!

If you have photocopied your source (a newspaper or magazine article, for instance), you can highlight main ideas with a brightly colored, transparent marker. Then when you make your note cards, you can go directly to the highlighted parts of the article.

 Exercise 6   Summarizing Important Information from a Source

Choose one of the sources that you plan to use for your research paper. On note cards or your computer, summarize each of the important ideas that may be of use to you, using your own words. Be sure to write a heading, the source number (see your bibliography cards), and the number of the page on which you found your information.

Here is a brief passage on the first African American baseball player in the major leagues. On a separate sheet of paper or your computer, take notes in your own words. The purpose of your research is to answer these two research questions: Who was the first African American baseball player in the major leagues? What happened to him? Compare your notes with those of a partner or small group.

When World War II ended, some people, including reporters, argued that African Americans had fought and died in the war and that it was time to integrate professional baseball. Branch Rickey, the Brooklyn Dodgers' president, agreed. He assigned Dodger scouts to search for a talented player in the Negro Leagues. Rickey chose Jackie Robinson, who was playing shortstop for the Kansas City Monarchs.

According to Rickey's plan, Robinson would play for a year with a Canadian team, the Montreal Royals, the Dodgers' best minor league team. In 1946, he led the league in batting and runs scored, and that year the Royals won the pennant and the Little World Series. The grateful Montreal fans considered him a hero.

On April 10, 1947, Rickey announced that Robinson would become the first African American player in the major leagues. That first season Robinson and his wife received hate mail and death threats. He and his teammates were jeered by fellow baseball players and managers and by fans. And Robinson was turned away from hotels and restaurants that accommodated his teammates. But Robinson never lost his cool, and he played extraordinary baseball that season. Lightning fast, he led the league in stolen bases. His 12 home runs, 175 hits, and great fielding at first base led to his being named Rookie of the Year. Robinson was named the Most Valuable Player in 1949, the year he stole 37 bases and led the league in batting.

When he was inducted into the Baseball Hall of Fame in 1962, Robinson said, "I feel quite inadequate to this honor. It is something that could never have happened without three people. Branch Rickey was as a father to me, my wife, and my mother. They are here making the honor complete." He became the first baseball player—black or white—to have his portrait on a U.S. postage stamp.

Exercise 8
Practice Taking Notes During an Interview

Pretend that you have been asked to introduce a classmate at a school assembly. Interview a classmate about his or her earliest memories, family, hobbies, ambitions, and so on. Think of five or six questions, and take notes on your classmate's responses. Introduce your classmate to the class, using the notes you took during your interview.

Exercise 9
Taking Notes for Your Research Paper

In each of the possible sources you have discovered, skim until you locate information you think will be useful in your research paper. Then take notes, following the guidelines on pages 46–47. You may end up with dozens of cards from each source. Before you leave each card, double-check to see that you have written the correct source number in the upper-right-hand corner and that you have listed the page numbers where you found the information.

Exercise 10
Checking Your Progress

Answer each of the following questions about the work you've done so far.

1. How are you doing in terms of your timetable (see page 9)? Are you on schedule? If not, what can you do to catch up?

   _____

   _____

2. What are the major headings in your working outline? Does your outline follow the form shown on page 43?

   _____

   _____

3. How did you decide when to take notes? How did you locate relevant information?

   _____

   _____

4. What essential information did you put on each of your note cards?

   _____

   _____

5. How have you distinguished direct quotations from your own notes, thoughts, and comments?

_____

_____

6. Explain the difference between a summary and a paraphrase. Have you used either of these on your note cards?

_____

_____

Checklist Review

☐ Before you start taking notes, make a working outline.

☐ Skim each source to locate information for your paper.

☐ Take notes in your own words.

☐ Enclose a direct quotation (the author's exact wording) in large quotation marks.

☐ Follow the guidelines for taking notes on pages 46–47.

☐ Make sure you give proper credit for a writer's words and ideas.

Write a Thesis Statement and a Title

CALVIN AND HOBBES © 1993 Watterson. Reprinted with permission of UNIVERSAL PRESS SYNDICATE. All rights reserved.

You have finished—or at least you think you've finished—taking notes. You have hundreds of note cards. What's next? You will be happy to know that the next few tasks are much easier than the ones you have already completed. You are now almost halfway through the job of writing a research paper. Check your progress against the schedule you have set for yourself.

Organizing and Evaluating Your Note Cards

Before you write a thesis statement and a title for your paper, you will need to pay some attention to your note cards.

☑ Sort your note cards into stacks having the same heading.

Some stacks will be short; some may be quite tall. If you have a great many cards under one heading, perhaps you should divide them into two or three more manageable subheadings.

Take time to reread each note card. Make sure that you have got the heading right. You may find cards that might better be classified under different headings.

☑ Evaluate your note cards.

If you stopped to read and evaluate information *before* you took notes from your sources, you probably will not have ended up with many unusable note cards. Some students, however, can't resist capturing every scrap of information that might just *possibly* turn out to be useful. Now is the time to get rid of what you are sure you will not use.

BE SELECTIVE. Do you have too much information on one subject? Use only the best—the most interesting, the most pertinent, the most persuasive. But do not destroy or throw away the weaker note cards; you may need them yet. Instead, place them at the bottom of the piles, and mark them in some way (maybe a small red X) so that when you start writing, you will recognize these cards as weaker than the others.

FILL IN THE GAPS. Is there not enough information in some stacks? Go back to the library, find more sources, and take additional notes.

REVISE YOUR OUTLINE. Revise your working outline to fit the information you have found. Consider eliminating any heading or subheading for which you have not been able to find enough information.

WHAT'S THIS DOING HERE? If you have no idea why a note card made it into a particular pile, move it to a more suitable pile, or drop it altogether. You might make a separate pile of possible discards.

Hint! You should end up with a stack of note cards for each heading and subheading in your working outline. If you don't have at least two cards for each section of the outline, you may not have enough information.

Exercise 1 Evaluating Your Notes

Ask yourself these questions about your note cards:

* Can I read what I wrote on each card?

* Does each card have a source number and a page number?

* Is every card directly related to a heading or subheading in my working outline?

* Do I have too little information for some headings?

* Do I have too much information for some headings?

* Does the information on the note card really fit the heading I have put it under? Do I need to move the card to a different heading or maybe discard it entirely?

On a separate sheet of paper or your computer, write a brief progress report. Mention any problems you have discovered as you evaluated your notes and what work still needs to be done.

E-writing If you have taken your notes on your computer, you should also have printed out a hard copy to work with. You can probably space out your computer notes so that three "note cards" fit on a page. Experiment until you get the spacing right. Then print all your notes, and cut each one to note-card size so that you can sort them into stacks having the same heading. You may end up with some combination of handwritten note cards and computer-printed notes. No problem. But there is still nothing like handling physical pieces of paper or note cards when you are trying to organize and evaluate your notes.

Unity

☑ Make sure that all your information fits the scope of your paper.

Think of the paper's **scope** as a big umbrella that covers all the paper's main ideas and supporting details. Information that strays outside the paper's scope distracts the reader and destroys the paper's **unity**. As you reread and evaluate your notes, you will develop an even clearer idea of exactly what you are writing about. If you suspect that a note card does not belong under the umbrella, pull it out and set it aside.

For example, if you are writing a research paper on the effects of day care on children under two years old, which of the following studies fit the paper's scope?

1. A study of children under the age of two who spend at least 20 hours a week in day-care centers in Houston, Texas

2. A recent study of the training, qualifications, and experience of day-care workers in New York City

3. A study of the personalities, development, and sleeping habits of 3,000 babies aged two or under who spend more than 10 hours a week in day care

4. A study of the personality differences in one-year-old identical twins in southern California

The first and third studies fit the paper's stated scope. The second and fourth studies do not. Study 2 is about day-care workers, not children in day care. Although study 4 deals with one-year-olds, it does not specify that these children are in day care.

Exercise 2 — What Fits and What Doesn't?

Put a check mark in the blank for the items of information that fit the research paper described. Write an X for the items that do not fit and will hurt the paper's unity.

For a research paper on the photographs of the Civil War taken by Mathew B. Brady and his assistants:

_____ 1. Brady's assistants took most Civil War photos; Brady almost blind

_____ 2. History of development of photography

_____ 3. Brady authorized to accompany Union troops and document war

_____ 4. Brady quote about going to Bull Run battlefield: "A spirit in my feet said 'Go' and I went."

_____ 5. Walt Whitman's poems about the Civil War

_____ 6. Brady's portrait photographs of Abraham Lincoln

_____ 7. Causes of the Civil War

Coherence

☑ Arrange the information in a way that readers will easily understand.

A paper is coherent when it is orderly and makes sense. You have already thought about ordering your ideas (as you wrote your working outline). Now it is time to check and rethink your organization. Arrange and rearrange your stacks of note cards until you are satisfied that the information flows in a logical way.

The three most common ways of ordering information are **chronological** (used to narrate the order of events in time), **spatial** (used to describe a place or object), and **by importance** (used to explain or to persuade). If you use order of importance, you can arrange ideas and details from most to least important or from least to most important. However, you do not have to force one of these types of organization onto your paper. Just concentrate on arranging ideas and details in the clearest, most natural, and most logical way.

Try explaining to a partner or small writing group why you have arranged the sections of your paper as you have, and ask for feedback.

Exercise 3 | **Ensuring Coherence**

Check your stacks of note cards against your working outline. Ask yourself the following questions.

* Now that I have sorted and evaluated my note cards, have I discovered any problems in my working outline? If so, how do I propose to fix these problems?

* What feedback have I received from a partner or writing group? What changes, if any, do I plan to make in response to this feedback?

On the lines below, write a brief progress report on any problems you have discovered and changes you plan to make.

_____

_____

_____

_____

Exercise 4 | **What's Wrong with This Working Outline?**

Work with a partner or small group to decide what's wrong with the following working outline. How would you suggest fixing the outline so that it is coherent and follows the proper outline form? You may find it helpful to review the outline form on page 43.

Chocolate

I. Growing cacao trees

   A. A tropical tree

II. Some great recipes

   1. My mother's recipes

   2. Others

III. Different types of chocolate

IV. Milk and dark chocolate

V. White chocolate

VI. Unsweetened chocolate for baking

VII. History of chocolate

VIII. How chocolate is made

Audience and Purpose

☑ Identify your audience and your purpose.

AUDIENCE. The manner in which you express your thesis statement and the way that you focus your paper depend in part on your intended audience. Imagine how a paper on the latest techniques for growing orchids might be tailored for each of the following audiences: members of an orchid club, a group of middle school students, a group of senior citizens who have no gardening experience, and a group of biology teachers.

Audiences vary in what they need to know and want to know. Some of the audiences mentioned would know a lot about growing orchids; some would know nothing. For audiences that know little, you would have to define terms and provide background information. For those who already know a lot about orchids and other plants, you could skip the background and discuss technical details.

Clearly, the primary audience for your research paper is your teacher and your classmates. But can you find a special audience, too? If you are writing about legislation and advertising designed to prevent teenagers from smoking cigarettes, for instance, you might make your paper available to the school's science club or to a local group of advertising professionals.

PURPOSE. If you have not already decided on the purpose of your research paper, now is the time to pin it down. Your purpose will affect which details you choose to include and the way you express your ideas. Are you trying to explain? Are you comparing and contrasting, analyzing causes and effects, or proposing a solution to a problem? Perhaps your purpose is to interpret or evaluate a literary work or works? Whatever your purpose, you will better maintain the focus of your paper if you always keep in mind the way in which you are trying to affect your audience.

Exercise 5 — Identifying Your Audience and Purpose

Stop to think about your research paper's audience and purpose. Answer each of the following questions in a complete sentence.

1. Who is the audience for my research paper?

   _____

   _____

2. What does my audience already know about the topic I am writing about? What might they need to know or want to know?

   _____

   _____

3. What other groups of people might be interested in this topic? How can I arrange to share my paper with them?

   _____

   _____

4. What is the purpose of my paper? (If possible, use one of the purposes mentioned on the preceding page, such as "analyze," "interpret," or "explain.")

   _____

   _____

Thesis Statement

☑ **Draft a working thesis statement that tells what you will cover in your paper.**

A thesis statement is a single declarative sentence that states the controlling idea of your research paper. It identifies both your topic and your limited focus and suggests what the body of your paper will cover. Usually, the thesis statement is either the first or the last sentence in the introductory paragraph.

Keep the following guidelines in mind as you draft your thesis statement.

* A thesis statement should not be expressed as a question. If you have phrased your limited topic as a research question, your thesis statement provides a one-sentence answer to that question.

* A thesis statement is a preview of what the paper is about. It states the topic and the writer's specific focus on the topic. (Do not begin with "The purpose of my paper is. . . ." or "In this paper, I will write about. . . .")

* A thesis statement controls the paper's content. Everything in the paper provides support for the thesis statement.

* A thesis statement may suggest, but should not state, your conclusions. Save your conclusions for the end of your paper.

* A thesis statement should have a confident tone. Sound as if you're sure of what you're saying. Avoid using hedge words and phrases such as *probably*, *might*, *I think*, *seems*, *apparently*, and *it seems to me*.

Here are several examples of faulty thesis statements. Note how each has been revised and improved.

EXAMPLE

Wordy and Tentative It seems to me that probably one of the seriously important decisions almost all teenagers face today is deciding what jobs they might have sometime in the future.	**Confident** The most important dilemma today's teenagers face is making informed career decisions: choosing a type of work that will sustain them and preparing adequately for that career.
Vague In this community crime is a problem that people can work together to overcome.	**Specific** Crime Watch, a community-based resident patrol, is a practical, effective way for citizens of all ages to cooperate in protecting themselves and their community from crime.
States Topic but Does Not Limit Focus Dogs can be trained to help disabled people.	**States Topic and Limits Focus** For thousands of disabled Americans, "service dogs" improve the emotional, social, and economic quality of life.
Question How can high school students start a school radio station?	**Statement** With as little as $500, high school students can create and staff a "drive-by" radio station, benefiting both the students and the school in significant ways.

Revising Thesis Statements

Read each of the faulty thesis statements that follow. Revise each thesis statement so that it meets the requirements stated in the guidelines on pages 59–60. You may make up details if you wish.

1. The purpose of my paper is to write about how strikes in sports have affected fans.

_____

_____

2. How do the amount and the kind of television that teenagers watch influence their achievements in school?

_____

_____

3. The purpose of my paper is to write about some of the many young-adult novels that deal with important issues that are helpful to their readers, who most likely never see counselors.

_____

_____

4. How do weather forecasters make their predictions?

_____

_____

5. I really think that something needs to be done about elections in the United States because too few people register to vote and usually only a small percentage of registered voters actually cast their ballots in local and state elections and even in the years when there are presidential elections.

_____

_____

Exercise 7 **Drafting a Thesis Statement for Your Paper**

Before you do this exercise, review your working outline and your stacks of note cards. Make sure you have a clear sense of the scope of your paper. Then, on a separate sheet of paper or your computer, write at least three significantly different versions of a thesis statement for your research paper. Choose the thesis statement you like best. Share all your thesis statements with a partner or writing group. Do your preferences match? Try to explain why the one you have chosen is the best.

Writing a Title

☑ **Draft a working title that reveals your topic and your narrowed focus.**

Your title is the first chance you have to communicate your topic and your focus (the limited part of the topic you're tackling) to your reader. A good title should mention both.

Although you are far from having to finalize your title, a working title and thesis statement will help clarify your thinking and keep you on track as you prepare your final outline (Step 5) and write the first draft of your paper (Step 6).

Keep the following guidelines in mind as you draft your working title.

* A straightforward title is better than one that is cute or too clever. The title should not leave your reader wondering, "What's that about?"

* A colon is helpful. You might write the topic first, followed by a colon, followed by your limited focus.

* The title should not be stated as a complete sentence, although it might suggest a question.

Here are some examples of faulty titles. Note how each has been revised and improved.

EXAMPLE

Too Vague Credit Card Problems	**Specific** Using Credit Cards: How to Keep from Going Under
Statement Too Many Children Don't Know What to Do in a Fire	**Revised** Teaching Children What to Do in a Fire
Too General Mystery Novels and Movies	**Specific** Making a Mystery Novel into a Movie: Successes and Failures
Unclear Feeding the Diet Industry	**Clear** The Diet Industry in America: Big Money
Too Cute Escaping with the Wizard of Oz	**Straightforward** Ballooning as a Sport: Advantages and Disadvantages

Exercise 8 **Revising Titles**

This exercise will give you some practice before you tackle your own title. Clearly, it is difficult to write a good title for a paper you know nothing about, but see what you can do with these titles. Make up whatever you need (usually a focus) to improve the title. Then get together with a small group to compare and discuss your revisions.

1. The United Nations

2. Creativity Should Be Encouraged

3. TV's Greatest Hits

4. Special Effects

5. Edgar Allan Poe

6. Diets for Staying Alive

7. Teenagers and Cars

8. Popular Music

9. Freedom of Speech

_____

_____

10. Buying Online

_____

_____

Exercise 9 | **Drafting a Title for Your Research Paper**

On a separate sheet of paper or your computer, write some titles (at least four) for your paper. Discuss them with a partner or writing group. Choose the one you like best. This can be your working title, and you can change it up until the day you turn your paper in.

Exercise 10 | **Checking Your Progress**

Answer each of the following questions about the work you've done so far.

1. Check the timetable on page 9. Do you need to speed up, or are you on schedule?

_____

_____

2. What general headings have you used to stack or group your note cards?

_____

_____

3. Do you have too much or too little information in any of your stacks of note cards? What will you do to solve this problem?

_____

_____

4. Which note cards have you discarded? Why?

_____

_____

5. What is your working thesis statement? What is your working title?

_____

_____

Checklist Review

☐ Sort your note cards into stacks having the same heading.

☐ Evaluate your notes. If you have too much information under a heading, discard the least interesting notes. If there's not enough information under a heading, find more sources and take notes.

☐ Revise your working outline to fit the information you have found.

☐ Make sure that all the information fits the scope of your paper.

☐ Arrange the information in an order that readers can easily understand.

☐ Identify your audience and your purpose.

☐ Draft a working thesis statement that tells what you will cover in your paper.

☐ Draft a working title that reveals your topic and your narrowed focus.

Write a Final Outline

Reprinted by permission: Tribune Media Services

The last step before you actually start writing your paper is finalizing your outline. If you did a working outline in Step 3, you will need to update and revise it now. But the writing process isn't exactly the same for everyone. You may be a writer who writes first and outlines later. Check with your teacher to see if it's okay to postpone—but not omit—the outline step until after you write your first draft. Keep in mind also that some teachers do not require a formal outline. Ask your teacher whether you will have to submit one.

Content and Organization

Your final outline shows at a glance the two essential aspects of your paper: its content and its organization. Usually, a final outline includes a third element, your thesis statement, which comes right after the title and before the outline of the body of the paper.

The three important parts of a research paper that *never* appear in an outline are the introductory paragraph(s), the paper's conclusion or concluding paragraph(s), and the Works Cited list. You will learn more about these parts of your paper in Step 6 and Step 7.

Hint!

Some teachers do not want the thesis statement to appear in the outline. Find out whether your teacher wants the thesis statement included.

☑ Choose either a topic outline or a sentence outline.

Your outline must be either a topic outline or a sentence outline, not a combination of both. You cannot mix the two types of outlines. Your teacher may make the decision for you by specifying which type you will be required to write.

In a topic outline, the headings and subheadings are a series of words or phrases, not complete sentences.

I. Native American "code talkers" during World Wars I and II
   A. Who they were
      1. Their tribes
      2. Their languages
   B. What they did
   C. Why they were so successful
      1. Spoken (not written) languages
      2. Languages totally unfamiliar to enemy code breakers

In a sentence outline, every heading and subheading is a complete sentence. (A complete sentence contains a subject and a verb and expresses a complete thought.)

Hint!

Each type of outline has its advantages. A topic outline is quicker and easier to write. A sentence outline takes more time but has two distinct points in its favor: (1) It furnishes ready-made topic sentences for your paragraphs. (2) Because it forces you to summarize what you are going to say about each topic, it can reveal problems in the organization of your ideas.

I. Native Americans served successfully as "code talkers" in the United States Armed Forces during World Wars I and II.
   A. They were fluent speakers of their native languages.
      1. They were Choctaw, Navajo, Comanche, Winnebago, Kiowa, and Cherokee.
      2. Each tribe spoke a unique language.
   B. Code talkers transmitted military information via walkie-talkie radios and field telephones to other speakers of their language.
   C. Enemy code breakers were unable to understand the American Indians' languages.
      1. Almost all were spoken languages only and had no written form.
      2. These tribal languages were totally unfamiliar to outsiders.

The Form and Logic of an Outline

☑ **Follow the correct outline form.**

The main headings and subheadings are written in a standard form.

❋ A number or letter precedes each heading. Each number or letter is followed by a period or is enclosed in parentheses.

❋ The first word in every heading begins with a capital letter. Sentence outlines (but *not* topic outlines) have a period at the end of each heading.

❋ Indentations show a heading's level of importance. An indented heading is a subdivision of the preceding heading.

> Title of Paper
>
> Thesis statement:_____.
>
> I. Main heading
>
>   A. First-level subheading
>
>   1. Second-level subheading
>
>   2. Second-level subheading
>
>   a. Third-level subheading
>
>   b. Third-level subheading
>
>   (1) Fourth-level subheading
>
>   (2) Fourth-level subheading
>
>   (a) Fifth-level subheading
>
>   (b) Fifth-level subheading
>
>   B. First-level subheading
>
>   etc.

☑ **Identify the major sections of your paper. These will be your main (Roman numeral) headings.**

How can you figure out what the main headings of your outline should be? If you did a working outline to help guide your note-taking (Step 3), you have already made a stab at identifying the main headings and subheadings. Compare your stacks of note cards (separated according to headings) with your working outline. Do you want to change some of the main headings or reword them? Do you want to add new main headings? Do you want to drop some of the main headings?

Hint!

How many main headings should you have? At least three and no more than five. If you do not have enough main headings, or if you have too many, rethink the organization of your paper.

When you are figuring out your main headings and subheadings, you are using the critical-thinking skill of **analysis**: That is, you are breaking your topic into its smaller, separate parts. (When you analyze something, you break it into its separate parts and examine each part. For example, you analyze a short story by discussing its plot, characters, point of view, setting, and theme.)

Throughout your outline, make sure that headings and subheadings are **discrete**—that is, entirely separate. Headings and subheadings should not overlap or duplicate each other. There are two things wrong with the main headings in the following example. Can you find them both?

ILLOGICAL

Topic: Why the movie *The Wizard of Oz* remains an enduring classic

    I. Its plot

    II. Its story line

    III. Its music

    IV. Its visual effects and songs

Main headings I and II are about the same thing (plot and story line mean the same thing), and the "songs" part of heading IV duplicates the "music" of heading III.

LOGICAL

Topic: Why the movie *The Wizard of Oz* remains an enduring classic

    I. Its plot

    II. Its characters

    III. Its music

    IV. Its special effects

Here are four common types of research papers with examples of how the topic has been broken up into main headings.

1. **Examine a problem. Discuss one or more solutions.**
   Topic: How to reduce school violence

       I. Statistics past and present

       II. Solution 1: school crime-watch organization

       III. Solution 2: peer mediation program

       IV. Solution 3: increased security

2. **Examine an effect. Discuss several causes.**
   Topic: What has caused the greenhouse effect, and how serious is it?

       I. Increased burning of fossil fuels (coal, gas, oil) produces increases in carbon dioxide and other greenhouse gases.

       II. Even small environmental changes may lead to significant global warming.

       III. Clouds may either raise or lower Earth's temperatures.

3. Examine a cause. Discuss several effects.

   Topic: Regular exercise and a low-fat diet

    I. Decrease in heart disease

    II. Decrease in obesity

    III. Increase in average life span

4. History of something (a movement, an event, an idea)

   Topic: The essay, a relatively new literary form

    I. First essays (French lawyer and scholar Michel de Montaigne, 1533–1592)

    II. Formal essays (e.g., Ralph Waldo Emerson, 1803–1882)

    III. Informal essays (20th century)

Exercise 1   **Analyzing a Topic to Formulate Main Headings**

Use your imagination and common sense to write three or four main headings that might be covered in a research paper on each of the numbered topics. (NOTE: There are no right answers to this exercise, only different approaches to analyzing the topic.) Work with a partner or in a small group, and compare your main headings with those of your classmates.

1. How to increase voter turnout in the United States

    I. _____

    II. _____

    III. _____

    IV. _____

2. How cell phones have changed American life

    I. _____

    II. _____

    III. _____

    IV. _____

3. The three (or four) best things about television

    I. _____

    II. _____

    III. _____

    IV. _____

4. How advertisers persuade you to buy their products

I. _____

II. _____

III. _____

IV. _____

Exercise 2   **Identifying the Main Headings in Your Research Paper**

Write your topic and the working title of your research paper. On the lines below, divide your paper into at least three main headings.

Topic _____

Working Title _____

I. _____

II. _____

III. _____

IV. _____

☑ **Divide the main headings into subheadings and then into sub-subheadings, as needed. You can never have only one subheading; you must have at least two.**

It is not logical to divide a larger heading into only one subheading. (Think of dividing a whole pie into pieces: You can cut the pie many different ways, but unless you have at least two pieces, you have not divided the pie.)

Here is part of an outline showing subheadings and sub-subheadings:

EXAMPLE

```
Topic: Why the movie The Wizard of Oz remains an enduring
       classic
  I. Its plot
     A. Frame of story
        1. Tornado in Kansas
        2. Return to Kansas
     B. Fantastic adventure
     C. Suspenseful conflicts
        1. Good versus evil
        2. Struggle to return home
 II. Its characters
     A. Girl as hero
     B. Sympathetic scarecrow, tin man, lion
```

☑ Within any level, word the headings so that they are parallel in structure.

In writing, *parallel* means having the same grammatical structure. In the following example, the headings in A, B, and C are parallel. Each heading is made up of a noun followed by an infinitive phrase ("to" plus a verb).

> II. Instruments to predict volcanic eruptions
>
>   A. Chemical sensor to analyze gases in volcanic plume
>
>   B. Seismometer (buried sensor) to record vibrations in magma
>
>   C. Sensors to measure cracks in volcano's surface

In the following example, the A, B, and C headings are not parallel.

> II. Instruments to predict volcanic eruptions
>
>   A. Chemical sensor for measuring gases in volcanic plume
>
>   B. How a seismometer (buried sensor) is used
>
>   C. Cracks on surface

Hint!

Try this "bottom-up" technique to check the logic of your outline: Read the outline from the bottom up. Each group of lesser subheadings should "add up" to the more important heading above it.

Exercise 3 Parallel Structure

Revise the headings in the following outlines to make them parallel. (Write your corrections on the page.) Compare your revised headings with a partner's.

```
1. Topic: Jane Addams and her work

   I. About Jane Addams's life

  II. 1889, helped found Hull House, a settlement house
      in Chicago.

 III. Addams had other interests.

        A. Her work for women's rights

        B. Winning the Nobel Peace Prize
```

```
2. Topic: Animated cartoons: The technology

   I. Artists who draw cartoons by hand

      A. Summary of what makes cartoon characters move

      B. Earliest short cartoons

      C. In Walt Disney studios, the famous group of animators
         —the Nine Old Men—who created full-length movies
         such as Bambi, Peter Pan, 101 Dalmatians.

   II. Animation done by computers

      A. How it works

      B. Tron (1984), first computer-animated film

   III. What is the future of animated cartoons?
```

GUIDELINES

Writing a Final Outline

* Write either a sentence outline or a topic outline. *Don't mix the two types.*

* A number or letter precedes each heading. Each number or letter is followed by a period or enclosed in parentheses.

* Every heading begins with a capital letter. Sentence outlines (but not topic outlines) have a period at the end of each heading.

* Indentations show a heading's level of importance. An indented heading is a subdivision of the preceding heading.

* If any heading calls for subheadings, there must be two or more.

* The wording of headings within a section must be parallel.

Exercise 4 | **What Might the Headings Be?**

The note cards in this exercise are for a report on the development of skyscrapers and their effects on the people who live and work in them. The thesis statement for the report is: Two American inventions—steel-frame construction and a safety device for elevators—led to the skyscraper, which altered Earth's human landscape. Read the notes carefully. Then, on a separate sheet of paper or your computer, develop an outline based on them. Try to make your headings and subheadings logical and parallel. Meet with several classmates to talk about your outlines based on these notes.

History of skyscrapers—Chicago   1

Before skyscrapers, masonry (brick or stone) construction—
thick walls at base to support upper stories

Chicago fire Oct.8–10, 1871, destroyed 3 1/2 mi. central city →
building boom

Steel—frame construction (unlike masonry) allowed windows,
more room @ base, greater number of stories

1st skyscraper = 9—story Chicago's Home Insurance Co. Bldg.
1884–85, architect Major Wm. LeBaron Jenney, "father of
the skyscraper" Anecdote: Jenney got steel—frame
construction idea when wife put heavy book on top of metal
birdcage—thin wires supported it

Great Chicago architect—Louis Henry Sullivan.

                                                    pp. 539–541

Importance of Elevator   1

Essential invention—elevators

In NYC, Elisha Graves Otis (1811–1861) invented
safety device: stopped elevator from falling if
chain broke; 1st passenger elevator 1857

Otis patented device in 1861, built steam elevators
"vertical railways"—used esp. in hotels; later
powered by electric motors

                                                    pp. 537–538

History of word "skyscraper"   2

1794—triangular sail on a clipper ship; original
meaning

1826—high—standing horse

1857—very tall man

1892—person riding a high cycle

1891—tall building of many stories; first use in
Boston Massachusetts Journal

Effects of skyscrapers   3

Residential and business skyscrapers: treat
separately?
Some effects: growth of cities as centers of
commerce, greater population density, less human
scale (no neighbors, no sense of community)
Positive: great views, lots of light, efficient use
of city's limited space
Negative: "too impersonal," hate waiting for
elevators

pp. 430-431

What Lewis Mumford says   3

"If fast transportation made the horizon the limit
for urban sprawl, the new methods of construction
made the 'sky the limit,' as gamblers loved to say."
Acc. to Mumford, urban density "befouled &
poisonous air, constricted housing, demoralized
social life, teeming with violence & crime"

pp. 430-431

What workers say   4

Survey of people who work in skyscrapers
Their fears (safety: dependence on elevators &
electricity; dangerous in earthquake & fire)
Convenient to fast public transportation

Exercise 5 — Revising Your Working Outline

Spend some time looking over your note cards and your working outline. As you do
so, ask yourself each of the following questions. (You may want to write down your
answers on a separate sheet of paper or your computer.) They will help you to
decide what changes you will need to make in your outline.

* Which headings or subheadings need more information?

* Are there headings or subheadings that need to be added?

* Are there headings or subheadings that should be dropped?

* Which headings or subheadings need to be changed or reworded?

* What other changes do I need to make?

On the lines below, write your final outline. Use a separate sheet of paper if you need more room.

_____

_____

_____

_____

_____

_____

_____

_____

_____

_____

_____

_____

_____

_____

_____

_____

_____

_____

_____

_____

_____

_____

_____

_____

_____

_____

_____

_____

_____

_____

Answer each of the following questions about the work you've done so far.

1. What problems did you encounter when you were trying to finalize your outline?

_____

_____

2. How did you solve those problems?

_____

_____

3. How did you improve your outline?

_____

_____

4. How are you doing in terms of your timetable (see page 9)? If you are not on schedule, what do you need to do to catch up?

_____

_____

Checklist Review

☐ Choose either a topic outline or a sentence outline.

☐ Follow the correct outline form.

☐ Identify the major sections of your paper. These will be your main (Roman numeral) headings.

☐ Divide the main headings into subheadings and smaller subheadings as needed. You can never have only one subheading; you must have at least two.

☐ Within any level, word the headings so they are parallel in structure.

Write a First Draft

You have passed the halfway mark in the writing of your research paper. You have your note cards and (probably) a final outline. You have drafted a thesis statement and a working title. Now you need to pull it all together in sentences and paragraphs. You will use the critical-thinking skill called *synthesis*. Synthesis is the putting together of all kinds of pieces and parts and creating something new. For a research paper you start out with lots of raw material—notes about other people's ideas—and you end up with something unique: a paper that is different from anything that anybody has ever written before.

What You Do Not Have to Do

Let's start with five things you *don't* have to do when you draft your paper.

1. You don't absolutely have to have a final outline before you start drafting. You may be one of those write-first, outline-later people who asks, "How do I know what I'm going to write until I see what I've written?"

2. You don't have to write the introduction, body, and conclusion in that order. Some people write from the beginning to the end of the paper. Other writers draft the body first and leave the introduction and conclusion until last.

3. You don't have to write the body of your paper in the order shown in your outline. Just start with the main idea that you feel most confident about. Draft that whole Roman numeral section. Then pick another section to attack.

4. You don't have to think about niceties. You need not worry too much about writing perfectly formed sentences at this step. You will have plenty of time for all that later when you revise (Step 8). For the moment just focus on getting your ideas onto paper or your computer screen.

5. You don't have to panic. If you discover that something is lacking or otherwise amiss, it is not too late to fix it.

Some General Guidelines

Since the writing process is different for everyone, there is no fixed set of rules you must follow as you draft your paper. You may follow the suggestions here, or you may do it your own way. Just make sure that you do not put off drafting and that you leave yourself plenty of time to do a good job when it comes time to revise and put your paper in final form.

1. Writing your first draft is a big task, but it is just a beginning. Remember, nothing is chiseled in stone. You will make lots of changes (see Step 8) before you are done.

2. Try to write your first draft in one sitting, without interruption. Find a quiet place and stay focused until you have finished. If you cannot finish in one sitting, try to do it in two or three sessions.

3. Follow your outline, but adjust it as needed. If something just doesn't work, drop it. If something needs to be put in, add it.

4. Write in the third person. (Do not mention yourself; do not use the pronouns *I* or *me* or *we*). This will give your paper an objective, factual tone.

5. Find your own voice. Express your ideas as clearly and directly as you can. Do not use fancy-sounding words that you cannot define.

6. Give credit! Do not pass off anyone else's words or ideas as your own. Keep very careful track of your sources, and be sure to document them.

7. Save everything. Do not throw out any of your note cards or (if you have taken notes on a computer) note card documents.

E-writing Be sure to save your work at regular intervals (every 5 minutes or so) or set your computer's autosave function so that you do not risk losing what you have written if there is a power failure or a computer malfunction.

Writing an Introduction

☑ **Write an introduction that attracts your reader's attention and clearly indicates what your paper will be about. Include your thesis statement somewhere in your introduction.**

For a long research paper, your introduction may take one paragraph or several. Often the thesis statement is the first or last sentence of the introduction. It points the way to the body of your paper, indicating the main ideas you will cover there. Your introduction should also provide background information and define any key terms that readers need to know.

There is no single correct way to introduce your topic. You could probably write five or six distinct and equally effective introductions. In fact, it is a good idea to draft several entirely different approaches and choose the one you like best. Here are some tried-and-true ways that you might consider (but if you come up with something better, by all means use it).

Hint!

When you write your introduction: (1) Don't try to be funny. (2) Don't repeat the title. (3) Don't state your purpose: "The purpose of this paper is . . ."

* Tell a brief story (an anecdote).

* Describe a problem or condition.

* Ask a question.

* Cite some startling or interesting fact or statistic.

* Use a powerful or intriguing quote.

In Step 10 you'll find a model research paper entitled "Lacrosse: Yesterday and Today." The writer begins his paper with a comparison of lacrosse and three familiar sports. He uses these comparisons to capture the reader's attention. The writer's thesis statement is the last sentence in the paragraph.

EXAMPLE

```
If you go to a lacrosse game today, you will see a fast-
moving, rough sport that resembles soccer, ice hockey, and
football. Like hockey, lacrosse is a stick-and-ball game
in which players manipulate the ball/puck without touching
it with their hands. As in hockey and soccer, players try
to score points by advancing the ball/puck past a defend-
ing goalie and into the opposing team's net-shaped goal.
As in all three sports, they struggle fiercely to prevent
their opponents from scoring. Like all three sports,
lacrosse is an aggressive game with teams charging up and
down a field. However, as exciting as it is to watch or
play lacrosse today, it cannot compare with the earliest
games of lacrosse played by Native Americans.
```

E-writing If you have written notes on your computer, copy them into the document that you are using for your first draft. You can copy and paste quotations and other ideas where they belong in your draft (in the appropriate paragraph). Then you can reword them or incorporate them into your own sentences. Be sure to use your own words and to give credit to the original source.

If you're quoting from a source, double-check to make sure that you've got the quotation exactly right and that you've enclosed the sentence or phrase in quotation marks.

 **Exercise 1**   Analyzing an Introduction

Read each of the following two introductions to papers comparing two literary works. Then, on a separate sheet of paper or your computer, answer each of the questions. Meet with a partner or small group to talk about your answers.

> At first glance, it is difficult to see any similarities between Alice's adventures in Wonderland and those of the central character in Hermann Hesse's Siddhartha. Alice's adventures are those of a young girl in a world of imagination and nonsense. Siddhartha tells of the quest of an Indian boy for spiritual fulfillment. However, when we look at the underlying messages in these books, it becomes clear that what the main characters experience is very much alike. Their journeys, so different on the surface, merge into one path. The similarities of Alice's and Siddhartha's adventures can be shown through examination of the characters, their situations, and the novels' symbols.

> What does the white whale represent? What are the various humorous techniques that Mark Twain uses? All the attention focused on questions such as these tends to obscure other important elements of Moby Dick and Roughing It. These two texts are travelogues; that is, they are records of the places, animals, and people found on journeys into strange and unknown frontiers. The main characters of both books receive an education about the world around them, about other cultures and modes of living; but in doing so, they also receive a thorough education about the values and assumptions of their own society.

1. From the introductions, can you identify the three main sections (Roman numeral headings) of the research papers? What do you think they are?

2. What, if anything, do you think the writers might do to improve the introductions?

Exercise 2   Writing an Introduction

On a separate sheet of paper or your computer, draft a one- or two-paragraph introduction based on the notes that follow. (The information on the note card is taken from *Solving Your Child's Reading Problems* by Ricki Linksman, who is the director of the National Reading Diagnostics Institute. The book was published in 1993 by Carol Publishing Group, New York.) You may make up any details you need. Read your introduction aloud, and then discuss it with a group of classmates.

Kids with Reading Problems   2
Ways to teach young children alphabet & sounds of letters; 4
different types of learning w. suggestions for activities:
1. visual—look for food labels, make collage of newspaper
   letters
2. auditory (hearing)—make up song, sentences w. words
   begin. w. sound
3. tactile (touch)—finger-paint letters; use glue & macaroni,
   sand, sparkles to make letter shapes
4. kinesthetic (motion)—outline letter w. chalk & have kid
   walk the letter
                                                        pp. 130–135

Exercise 3 **Drafting Your Introduction**

On a separate piece of paper or your computer, draft two or three entirely different introductions for your research paper. Share these introductions with a small group of classmates, and ask for feedback. Decide on the introduction you like best.

Writing the Body of Your Paper

☑ **Keep very careful track of your sources. Insert your bibliography source card number after ideas or quotations that need to be acknowledged.**

This is the point where documenting sources can go awry and the possibility of accidental plagiarism occurs. As you review your note cards, watch for those large quotation marks that alert you to a direct quotation. Pay careful attention to ideas that need documenting, too. Plug in parentheses and source card numbers at the appropriate spots. (You will learn all about **parenthetical citation** in Step 7.)

☑ **Write in the present tense. Use the past tense only to refer to historical events.**

This advice about tenses follows the MLA (Modern Language Association) style, which is preferred by most high school teachers. Even though a work of literature was written long ago, it still exists, so the present tense is used to discuss it.

Here are some examples that show the correct use of present and past tense according to MLA style.

EXAMPLE

PRESENT TENSE	In "I heard a Fly buzz—when I died—" Emily Dickinson **describes** what the speaker in the poem **feels** at the moment of death.
PRESENT TENSE	In his *Philosophiae naturalis principia mathematica* (1687), Sir Isaac Newton **describes** his laws of universal gravity.
PAST TENSE	In 1901, Beatrix Potter **published** *The Tale of Peter Rabbit* privately.
PAST TENSE	Sir Isaac Newton **built** a reflecting telescope in 1668.

☑ Each paragraph in the body should include a topic sentence that states a main idea. The rest of the sentences should provide supporting details.

Topic sentences perform two useful functions in informative, or expository, writing—the kind of writing you are doing in a research paper. A **topic sentence** states the paragraph's main idea and also controls the paragraph's content. All the other sentences in the paragraph should support the topic sentence, offering convincing evidence or proof. Try to provide information from at least two different sources to support each topic sentence.

In each of the two paragraphs below, the first sentence is the topic sentence. (The parenthetic citations are to the writer's source cards.)

Sandra Cisneros's prize-winning novel, The House on Mango Street (1984), is unusual in that it combines different genres (1). It reads like an autobiography, but it is fiction, which makes it a fictional autobiography. Most critics agree that The House on Mango Street is a "Bildungsroman," a German word for a novel about a young person's growing to maturity. The narrator is Esperanza Cordero, who observes her family and friends "in a lyric narrative voice" (2). The novel contains forty-four very short narratives, or literary sketches; some call them vignettes (3). Each of these sketches reads like a miniature short story, and many have been anthologized as separate pieces. Cisneros recalls that her goal in writing The House on Mango Street was to write stories that combined poetry and fiction:

I wanted to write a collection which could be read at any random point without having any knowledge of what came before or after. Or that could be read in a series to tell one big story. I wanted stories like poems, compact and lyrical and ending with a reverberation. (1)

Although it is rooted in the Mexican-American community of Chicago, where Cisneros herself grew up, <u>The House on Mango Street</u> has a universal theme: the quest for identity. In the novel, the young narrator is "struggling to find a place in her community without relinquishing her sense of self" (3). Esperanza observes the women and girls around her and realizes that "one way to leave house and barrio is to acquire an education" (1). Like Alicia in the vignette "Alicia Who Sees Mice," Esperanza wants something more than to be a wife and mother rolling tortillas. She wants to become a writer.

 Exercise 4 **What's Wrong with This Paragraph?**

Get together with a partner to talk about this paragraph from the body of a research paper.

Many primates have been trained to perform as humans do. I've seen them often, in circuses, in shows, and in movies. You probably have, too. Three out of every five chimpanzees can be trained, while two out of every five orangutans can. Without too much labor and a great deal of difficulty, orangs can sit at a table, eat and drink like humans, ride a tricycle or bicycle, dress themselves, open a lock with a key and even pick the right key out of a half dozen or more, and pound nails with a hammer. One orang learned how to pedal and ride a tricycle in only three lessons—much faster than a small child usually learns.

1. What do you think this research paper is about?

_____

_____

2. What is the topic sentence of this paragraph?

_____

_____

3. Does the paragraph provide enough support for its topic sentence? How many different kinds of support are given?

_____

_____

4. Tell why you do or do not believe the writer's facts and statistics. What is missing from this paragraph?

_____

_____

Exercise 5   **Writing a Paragraph**

On a separate sheet of paper or your computer, use the information in the following note cards to write one paragraph for the body of a research paper. (On the note cards, the abbreviation "Q." stands for Quetzalcoatl.) The title is: The Legends of Quetzalcoatl and King Arthur. The thesis statement is: The ancient Mexican god Quetzalcoatl and the legendary English King Arthur are similar in startling ways.

Legend of Quetzalcoatl   3
Portrayed as plumed (feathered) serpent; the Toltec (pre-
Aztec Mexican people) god who gave corn, learning, arts.
Q. also an actual ruler—sent into exile when high priests
disgraced him, in conflict with sky god.
"Q. the ruler eventually became identified with the god, and
his story is a mixture of history and legend."
Legend of his promise to return important to Aztecs, 16th c.:
Exiled from Tula; made a raft of serpents & set off across
sea; vowed to return to reclaim his throne in year called 1
Reed.
(My note: Something like King Arthur's leaving on a boat,
vowing to return when Britain is in need. Is Q. like King
Arthur? Compare & contrast them?)
                                                    pp. 19–20, 25

                                                                3

         Warburton, Lois. Aztec Civilization. World History
         Ser. San Diego, CA: Lucent Books, 1995.

Legend of Quetzalcoatl   5
Q's rivalry with Tezcatlipoca, war god. Q. = "Father and
Creator, the source of agriculture, science, and the arts.
He was an enlightened god, the morning star and the evening
star."
Various versions of Q's death: sailed toward east on raft
of serpents; parted Gulf of Mexico's waters & walked away;
became morning star; smoke from funeral pyre; ➜ quetzal
birds. All have in common: prophecy that one day he would
return.

                                              pp. 75–76
[My note: see also 2-page mural of Q's life, pp.62–63 by
Mexican artist Diego Rivera.]

                                                          3

Josephy, Alvin M., Jr. 500 Nations. New York: Knopf, 1994.

Legend of King Arthur   6
Legendary Celtic warrior–king, 5th–6th c., who fought
Saxons
Reigned at Camelot w. knights of Round Table (A. & his
knights represented "ideal of medieval knighthood and
chivalry")
A. killed in battle, body borne away by boat to isle of Avalon;
prophecy of his return someday

                                                          6

The Columbia Encyclopedia. 6th ed. New York:
Columbia UP, 2001.

 Exercise 6   **Writing the Body of
Your Research Paper**

On separate sheets of paper or your computer, draft the body of your
research paper.

Writing the Conclusion

Here is a common mistake: You are so glad to be finished with the body of your paper that you lose momentum and concentration, and your paper ends with a thud. Avoid this mistake by spending just as much time working on your conclusion as you did on the introduction.

☑ **Write a conclusion that brings your paper to a satisfying close and says something worthwhile.**

Instead of just rephrasing your thesis statement, see if you can leave the reader with something to think about. Try these approaches:

* Offer a judgment.

* Make a final comment or observation.

* End with a quotation that pulls it all together.

* Summarize your main idea(s).

* Refer to your introduction.

In this concluding paragraph, the writer mentions several examples of media coverage at the time of the Cuban Missile Crisis and ends with a final comment, or judgment, about the events and their aftermath.

At the time of the Cuban Missile Crisis (October 1962), observers recognized that the crisis held tremendous significance for the United States and for the whole world. "The ships of the U.S. Navy were steering a course that would be marked boldly on the charts of history," Life magazine proclaimed. "The steel perimeter clamped around Cuba by the U.S. could be the trip-wire for World War III" (1). Newsweek predicted that the crisis "may turn out to have consequences of incalculable importance for this century" (2). Things could have turned out very differently than they did, but the prudence and caution of both President Kennedy and Soviet Premier Nikita Khrushchev turned this crisis into an opportunity for peace.

Here is a writer's conclusion for a research paper about the life and works of the American poet Theodore Roethke. Read the conclusion and then answer the questions that follow.

Theodore Roethke was a bold and brilliant poet whose explorations of nature and his own soul gave us some of the best and most unusual poetry in American literary history. His poetry was greatly influenced by his early years and is perhaps all the more searing because it cost him so much inside—cost him, at times, his very sanity. However, as Robert Boyers says:

> It is his triumph that his best poems permit us to embrace the principle of change as the root of stability; that his best poems, through rhythm and syntax and diction, so evoke passion that we are able actively to sympathize with his sense of loss; and that we can feel, with him, how all finite things reveal infinitude. (5)

In all these things, Roethke is truly unique. Theodore Roethke's poetry shows us the pattern of the universe by showing us the pattern on a leaf; he gives us a glimpse of himself, and in doing so gives us an unforgettable glimpse of ourselves and all mankind.

---

1. Based on this conclusion, identify the two main sections (Roman numeral headings) of the research paper.

_____

_____

2. Do you think this conclusion would be better or worse without the long quotation from Robert Boyers? Explain why you think so.

_____

_____

3. What, if anything, do you think the writer could do to improve this conclusion?

_____

_____

On a separate sheet of paper or your computer, write at least two diffe~~~~
sions. Read them aloud to several classmates, and ask for their feedba~~~~
decide on the one you think is best.

Using Direct Quotations

Some of your note cards probably contain direct quotations that you think you might use in your paper. As you were taking notes, you enclosed them in large quotation marks just to make sure you would know they are not your own words, and you also checked them carefully for accuracy.

☑ **Follow the conventions for using direct quotations. Make sure that you clearly identify the source of the quotation.**

In the examples that follow, the numbers in parentheses indicate the bibliographical source card number of the quote (and in poetry the line numbers also). These are temporary citations only. You will learn about **parenthetical citation** in Step 7.

Hint!

Do not use too many quotations (an overload gets boring), and keep them fairly brief. Also, do not keep quoting from a single source. Use a sprinkling of direct quotations from different sources.

PROSE QUOTATIONS

* Run prose quotations into the text if they are four typed lines or shorter.

At the beginning of a sentence

> "You gain strength, courage and confidence by every experience in which you really stop to look fear in the face," Eleanor Roosevelt writes (14).

At the end of a sentence

> Eleanor Roosevelt, who was painfully shy as a young woman, might have been writing about herself when she declared, "You gain strength, courage and confidence by every experience in which you really stop to look fear in the face" (14).

Interrupted quotation

> "You gain strength, courage and confidence," Eleanor Roosevelt writes, "by every experience in which you really stop to look fear in the face" (14).

* You do not have to quote whole sentences. Enclose words or phrases in quotation marks, and run them into your sentences.

> Ernesto Gallarza describes both the difficulties and
> kindnesses he experienced in the course of "the
> Americanization of Mexican me" (12).

* If a prose quotation is longer than four typed lines, set it off from the rest of the text. Start a new line and indent ten spaces from the left margin. Do not use quotation marks for these long quotes.

> Jane Austen sets the tone and theme of her comic novel
> Pride and Prejudice in its opening sentences:
>
> > It is a truth universally acknowledged, that a
> > single man in possession of a good fortune must be
> > in want of a wife. However little known the feel-
> > ings or views of such a man may be on his first
> > entering a neighborhood, this truth is so well
> > fixed in the minds of the surrounding families,
> > that he is considered as the rightful property of
> > some one or other of their daughters. (2)

QUOTATIONS FROM POEMS

* Run in three or fewer lines quoted from a poem and use a slash mark (/) to indicate the end of a line. Enclose the quoted lines in quotation marks. (The line numbers of the poem are shown in parentheses.)

> Walt Whitman's "Song of Myself" begins with these
> lines: "I celebrate myself, and sing myself,/ And what
> I assume you shall assume,/ For every atom belonging
> to me as good belongs to you" (1.1—3).

* When quoting more than three lines from a poem, write each line as it appears in the poem. Indent the quoted lines, and do not use quotation marks.

> In "The Raven," his most famous poem, Edgar Allan Poe
> bombards the reader with a whole gamut of sound
> effects to produce a chilling, hypnotic effect:
>
> > Once upon a midnight dreary, while
> >   I pondered, weak and weary,
> > Over many a quaint and curious
> >   volume of forgotten lore,
> > While I nodded, nearly napping,
> >   suddenly there came a tapping,
> > As of someone gently rapping,
> >   rapping at my chamber door.
> > "'Tis some visitor," I muttered,
> >   "tapping at my chamber door;
> >   Only this and nothing more." (1—6)

ELLIPSES AND BRACKETS

* Use an ellipsis (a series of three periods separated by spaces) to show where you have omitted words in a quotation. If the quotation comes at the end of a sentence, add a fourth period as end punctuation.

> In his introduction to A Tale of Two Cities, Shuckburgh compares Madame Defarge to Lady Macbeth, calling the Defarges "among the greatest—and most terrible—of Dickens's creations, perhaps of all...fiction."

> Charles Dickens begins A Tale of Two Cities with a description of the year 1775: "It was the best of times, it was the worst of times. It was the age of wisdom, it was the age of foolishness...."

* Use brackets to enclose words that you insert in a quotation in order to make the meaning clear.

> U.S. Senator William Fulbright told the Senate, "We are handicapped by [foreign] policies based on old myths rather than current realities" (12).

Exercise 9   Using Quotations

Write sentences that incorporate all or part of each quotation. Punctuate each quotation correctly. Use a separate sheet of paper or your computer if necessary.

1. "I have a dream that one day this nation will rise up and live out the true meaning of its creed: 'We hold these truths to be self-evident: that all men are created equal.' "

   —Dr. Martin Luther King, Jr., August 28, 1963, at the March on Washington, DC

   _____

   _____

   _____

   _____

   _____

   _____

2. Polonius, Laertes's father, saying farewell to his son:

   This above all: to thine own self be true,
   And it must follow, as the night the day,

Thou canst not then be false to any man.

—Act I, scene 3, lines 78–80, *Hamlet* by William Shakespeare

_____

_____

_____

_____

_____

3. "There are only two or three human stories, and they go on repeating them-selves as fiercely as if they had never happened before."

—Willa Cather (American novelist), in *O Pioneers!* Chapter 4, Part II [1913]

_____

_____

_____

_____

_____

_____

4. Two stanzas from "The Tiger":

When the stars threw down their spears,
And water'd heaven with their tears,
Did He smile His work to see?
Did He who made the lamb make thee?

Tiger, tiger, burning bright
In the forests of the night,
What immortal hand or eye
Dare frame thy fearful symmetry?

—William Blake (1757–1827) in *Songs of Innocence and Experience*

_____

_____

_____

_____

_____

_____

Exercise 10 | **Checking Your Progress**

Answer each of the following questions about the work you've done so far.

1. What did you attempt to do in your introduction? How might you improve the introduction?

   _____

   _____

2. How long did it take you to draft the body of your paper? How many sittings?

   _____

   _____

3. How many pages did you write? Do you feel that the body of your paper is about the right length? Too short? Too long?

   _____

   _____

4. In what order did you write the body of your paper? From beginning to end? Skipping around?

   _____

   _____

5. Did you follow your final outline? (Did you work from an outline?) Do you need to revise your outline?

   _____

   _____

6. Did you use all your note cards? Which ones did you not use, and why?

   _____

   _____

7. Did you write a topic sentence for every paragraph? Do you have adequate support for each topic sentence?

   _____

   _____

8. How pleased are you with the draft of the body of your paper? What work still needs to be done?

   _____

   _____

9. What did you attempt to do in your conclusion? How might you improve the conclusion?

_____

_____

10. Are you on schedule, ahead of schedule, or behind? (See the timetable on page 9.) What do you need to do next?

_____

_____

Checklist Review

☐ Write an introduction that attracts your reader's attention and clearly indicates what your paper will be about.

☐ Keep very careful track of your sources.

☐ Write in the present tense. Use the past tense only to refer to historical events.

☐ Every paragraph in the body should deal with a main idea, which is stated in its topic sentence. The rest of the sentences in the paragraph should provide adequate supporting details.

☐ Write a conclusion that brings your paper to a satisfying close and says something worthwhile.

☐ Follow the conventions for using direct quotations. Make sure that you clearly identify the source of the quotation.

Document Sources

PEANUTS reprinted by permission of United Feature Syndicate, Inc.

In Step 6 you completed the first draft of your research paper. Let it sit for a time while you do two tasks (parenthetical citations and your Works Cited list) that are important but less taxing than writing. In fact, this step, documenting your sources, is probably the easiest one of all. Check your progress against the timetable you have selected. Are you on schedule?

Parenthetical Citation

When you wrote your first draft, you carefully put your bibliography source card number in parentheses whenever you needed to give credit for a quote or an idea. This form of documentation was only temporary. Now it is time to do it the right way.

☑ Follow the style of documentation that your teacher specifies.

Most teachers prefer the MLA style of parenthetical documentation, which is the style followed in this book. (See Appendix C for a discussion of APA style.) A parenthetical citation is a shorthand reference to the Works Cited list at the end of your paper. It gives minimal information about a source (author's last name, page number on which the information was found), just enough for readers to locate the source in your Works Cited list.

Whenever you insert a parenthetical citation, you have two things to decide:

* where to place the citation
* what information belongs inside the parentheses

☑ Give credit for every quotation and paraphrase.

You will want to document accurately any words or ideas that you have borrowed, but it is not necessary to document common knowledge or every single sentence. Try not to overload your paper with citations. You can group ideas so that you cover a spread of pages in a single citation.

Here are some rules governing the placement and punctuation of citations.

Place a citation at a natural pause—that is, at the end of a sentence or after a phrase or clause.

```
"A turkey, for example, was worth a hundred seeds. A
small rabbit was worth thirty" (Burleigh [10]).
```

According to the *MLA Handbook*, the end of a sentence is preferred. However, a parenthetical citation should always come near the quotation or paraphrase it documents. Consequently, it may naturally fall somewhere in the middle of a sentence.

```
They were something like today's coaches (Vennum 28) ex-
cept that they had—or claimed to have—magical powers.
```

Place a citation at the end of a text sentence and before the end punctuation mark.

```
Unripe pods are green, but they change to yellow or
purple-red when they ripen (Burleigh [5]).
```

If a citation follows a quotation at the end of a sentence, place the citation after the final quotation marks and before the sentence's end punctuation.

```
Twenty-two-year-old Thomas Jefferson praised chocolate
as "superior to coffee or tea for health and nourish-
ment" (Beach 3).
```

A citation in the middle of a sentence comes before a comma, a colon, or a semicolon.

```
"A full-scale blockade generally has been interpreted
as an act of war," the Miami Herald reported
("Blockade"), and everyone feared what might happen.
```

For a long quote set off from the rest of the text, place the citation on the last line of the quote following the end punctuation mark. Follow this style for both prose and poetry.

```
Oren Lyons, honorary chairman of the Iroquois National
Lacrosse team, remembers:

     But I should mention that in 1890 the Iroquois
     were sanctioned against playing at all. Before that
     we were always part of the international games.
     We taught the English how to play, we taught the
     French how to play, we taught the Canadians and
     the Americans. We were quite active in the late
     1800s. We had three trips to England, played in
     front of Queen Victoria, and they couldn't beat us
     so they called us professionals and wouldn't allow
     us to play anymore. (Dellinger)
```

The form of the citation varies depending on the source. Use the following guidelines.

One author

Enclose in parentheses the author's last name and the page number where the quotation or idea can be found. Do not use any punctuation between the name and page number. Write the page number only. Do not use the word *page* or *pages* or the abbreviation *p.* or *pp.*

```
Canadians who settled in the northeastern states founded
lacrosse clubs in Baltimore, Boston, and Philadelphia
(Fisher 57).
```

If the author's name appears in the text, write only the page number in parentheses.

```
According to Hoyt-Goldsmith, players wore animal
charms, such as a hawk feather or bear claw, so that
the animal's spirit would help them during a game (13).
```

If you refer to a complete work, omit page numbers.

```
In 1990, almost thirty years after the crisis, the
government released a whole series of documents
directly related to the Cuban Missile Crisis (National
Security Archive).
```

More than one work by an author

Follow the styles shown in these examples:

```
Our first glimpse of the "metallic" Miss Murdstone
makes us fear for the young David (Dickens, David
Copperfield 46; ch. 4).
```

```
"It is a far, far better thing that I do, than I have
ever done," says Sydney Carton at the end of A Tale of
Two Cities (Dickens 380; ch. 15).
```

Two or more authors

If there are two authors, cite both authors' last names. Do not include the word *edited* or the abbreviation *ed.* in the citation.

```
Gradually, they darken from tan or white or light pink
to dark brown, and then they are packed in bags and
sold (McFadden and France 32-33).
```

If there are three or more authors, either cite every author's last name or use the first author's name followed by *et al.* ("and others"). Use the same style (authors' names or *et al.*) in your Works Cited list.

```
In philosopher Karl Popper's "open society," everyone
is free to criticize Government without fear of
punishment. It is the opposite of a totalitarian
society (Bullock, Stallybrass, and Trombley 608).
```

> In 1993, infectious diseases killed 16.5 million people worldwide, more than three times the number who died from cancer (Brown et al. 115).

No author

If no author is given, use the title or a shortened version of it (as given in the Works Cited list). Use quotation marks for the title of an article or editorial. Underline the title of a book.

> Carolus Linnaeus, a Swedish botanist, classified more than 4,400 species of animals and 7,700 species of plants ("Linnaeus").

Electronic sources

For an article accessed from an online subscription service (via a library), cite the author's last name or a title if no author is identified.

> Canadians popularized lacrosse and took it over (Taylor).

Another way to identify an electronic source is to include the information as part of a sentence.

> In his article "The Irony Hangs Thick at a Game of Lacrosse," Drew Hayden Taylor states that Canadians popularized lacrosse and took it over.

Cite the writer of an e-mail message. If the Works Cited list has two works by the same person, specify the e-mail message.

> Fearing nuclear attack, people descended on supermarkets for canned foods, water, candles, and batteries (Grunwald, e-mail).

Part of a work with many volumes

Cite the volume number followed by a colon and the page number(s). Don't write the words *volume* or *page*.

> In Contemporary Literary Criticism, many critics, among them American poets Stanley Kunitz and W. D. Snodgrass, comment on and analyze Roethke's poetry (8:455, 459).

To cite an entire volume in a parenthetical citation, write the author's name, a comma, the abbreviation *vol.*, and the volume number.

> The Gathering Storm is an authoritative account of the beginnings of World War II (Churchill, vol. 1).

Hint!

There is no set rule about when to include the author's name in a text sentence and when to refer to it only in the parenthetical citation. Either way is acceptable. Write what seems most natural to you. Your goal is simply to identify clearly the source of the quotation or paraphrase.

Two or more works in a single citation

Separate the citations with a semicolon.

Thirty years later, reporters interviewed and wrote about people who had played crucial roles in the crisis, among them U.S. General Curtis LeMay and journalist John Scali (Rhodes; Hernandez).

Quotation from an indirect source

If you are quoting from an indirect source, write the abbreviation *qtd. in* before the source. Whenever possible, however, try to quote from the original source. Sometimes, as in the following example, the original source is not available, and you have to credit an indirect source.

"Better to have met the issue squarely in Cuba," an editorial in the <u>Boston Herald</u> proclaimed, "than later in Berlin or Turkey or even Paris" (qtd. in "Excerpts").

Literary work

For prose works that appear in many different editions, cite the chapter (ch.), part (pt.), or section (sec.) number.

In Charles Dickens's <u>David Copperfield</u>, the villainous Uriah Heep threatens his employer, Mr. Wickfield, with what he knows: "Let sleeping dogs lie—who wants to rouse 'em? I don't. Can't you see I am as umble [humble] as I can be?" (ch. 39).

Cite the act and scene numbers of plays: (<u>Ham.</u> 2.1) or (<u>Ham.</u> II.i).

On hearing that his wife is dead, Macbeth grapples with the meaning of life:

> Life's but a walking shadow, a poor player
> That struts and frets his hour upon the
>   stage,
> And then is heard no more; it is a tale
> Told by an idiot, full of sound and fury,
> Signifying nothing. (<u>Mac.</u> 5.5)

Cite the line numbers of poems: ("Intimations" 1–4).

Roethke recalls his student Jane, who died when she was thrown from a horse, "And how, once startled into talk, the light syllables leaped for her,/ And she balanced in the delight of her thought" ("Elegy for Jane" 3–4).

Hint!

If you need to insert a citation that is not covered by any of these style rules, refer to the *MLA Handbook for Writers of Research Papers,* 6th edition.

Exercise 1 — What's Wrong with These Citations?

Fix them. Pay careful attention to placement, content, and punctuation. Write the sentence, with the citation, on a separate sheet of paper or your computer. (Hint: You will not need all the information given.)

1. Also, Alice and Siddhartha both went through an initiation, an increased aware-ness of the world. For Alice, it was when she realized that the Queen and her court were "nothing but a pack of cards" (this quote is in Chapter 12 of *Alice's Adventures in Wonderland*, which appears in many different editions), not authority figures to be respected and obeyed without question.

2. Anne Woods, the British television producer, is famous for having developed and produced an international hit TV series for preschoolers, Teletubbies. Now she has another show in the works, Boohbah. This is an exercise show aimed at preschool children. (I got this information from an article in the *New York Times Magazine*, January 4, 2004, pages 18+. The article is titled "She Speaks 3-Year-Old," and it was written by Susan Dominus.)

3. In "The Greek and Roman Writers of Mythology" (found on pages 21–23 in the preface to her classic *Mythology*), Edith Hamilton mentions some of the sources she uses for her lively retellings of ancient Greek myths (*Mythology* by Edith Hamilton in the Mentor paperback of the Little, Brown hardback edition, copy-right 1940 and 1942 by Edith Hamilton.)

4. A beautiful and exciting book of photographs and text called Eagle is intended, its author Terrence N. Ingram says, to give readers a close look at the lives of these magnificent birds. In his Introduction, Ingram states: "With their power, beauty, and strength, eagles have been considered a symbol of greatness by many different cultures throughout history." (*Eagle* by Terence N. Ingram was published by MetroBooks in New York. The quotation from the Introduction appears on page 12.)

Exercise 2 — Be a Peer Editor

Give this writer a hand by correcting all mistakes in parenthetical citations. Follow the MLA style of parenthetical documentation. This is a good exercise to do with a partner or small group if your teacher approves. (Hint: When a poem's title is men-tioned in the text, cite only line numbers.)

```
    The poetry of Theodore Roethke (1908–1963) has other

literary influences. Stanley Kunitz notes "throwbacks" to

nursery rhymes, folk literature, counting songs, the
```

Bible, and Blake. "But," he adds, "the poems, original and incomparable, belong to the poet and not his sources." (Stanley Kunitz, pages 102 and 103. A further influence is the poetry of both T. S. Eliot and W. B. Yeats. In Roethke's Words for the Wind, for instance, the poem "The Dying Man" is "in a voice almost indistinguishable from Yeats's" (W. D. Snodgrass, pp. 104–105). Some critics have attacked Roethke's imitation of Yeats, calling it a sign of weakness on Roethke's part and a lack of his own ideas and insight (Ralph J. Mills, Jr., page 30).

Roethke's poems are intensely personal. He takes the evolution of self as a theme in much of his poetry, occasionally relating it to another, or a beloved. (Pages 30 and 31 in Mills). An example of the self theme is found in the poem "Open House":

> My secrets cry aloud.
>
> I have no need for tongue.
>
> My heart keeps open house,
>
> My doors are widely swung.
>
> An epic of the eyes
>
> My love, with no disguise.

(These are lines 1–6 from the poem "Open House." I found this poem on page 718 in The New Oxford Book of American Verse, edited by Richard Ellmann, © 1976, Oxford University Press.)

Writing Parenthetical Citations

In the space provided write a parenthetical citation for the work or works given. Read each numbered item carefully before you write the citation. Much more information is provided than you will need. Provide only the information required, and be sure to enclose the citation in parentheses.

1. A reference to a brief feature called "You Be the Judge" by José Schorr. The article appears on page 82 of *Saturday Evening Post* in the March/April 2004 issue.

_____

2. An article entitled "Eskimo" on page 927 of *The Columbia Encyclopedia*, 6th edition, 2000. No author is listed.

_____

3. A quotation from a letter to the editor in *The Miami Herald*. The letter is by Frankie Ruiz and is titled "Successful Marathon." The letter appears on page 20 of Section A in the February 5, 2004, edition.

_____

4. A paraphrase of an idea in an article by Nicholas Confessore. The article is entitled "What Makes a College Good?" It appeared in *Atlantic Monthly* magazine on pages 118+ in the November 2003 issue of the magazine.

_____

5. *Women's Rights in the United States: A Documentary History*. The editors are Winston E. Langley and Vivian C. Fox. The citation refers to a chart near the beginning of the book, entitled "Significant Dates in the History of Women's Rights," which appears on pages xxxi–xxxiii.

_____

6. A reference to the entire book *The Diversity of Life* by Edward O. Wilson. *The Diversity of Life* was published in 1999 by W. W. Norton & Company.

_____

7. A quotation from *500 Nations: An Illustrated History of North American Indians* by Alvin M. Josephy, Jr., published in New York by Alfred A. Knopf in 1994. The reference is to material entitled "A Clash in the Arctic," pp. 173–181. Josephy's name appears in the sentence that ends with the citation.

_____

8. A quotation (lines 14–17) from a poem by Theodore Roethke entitled "Elegy for Jane." The research paper cites six other poems by Roethke.

_____

9. Reference to the entry for "Underground Railroad" on pages 1915–1918 of *Africana: The Encyclopedia of the African and African American Experience* edited by Kwame Anthony Appiah and Henry Louis Gates, Jr. The book was published in New York by Basic Civitas Books. It was copyrighted © 1999 by Kwame Anthony Appiah and Henry Louis Gates, Jr.

10. A four-line quotation from the beginning of Canto I (on page 3) of *The Inferno of Dante* by Dante Alighieri, in a new verse translation by the American poet Robert Pinsky. The book was published in New York in 1994 by Farrar, Straus and Giroux.

Exercise 4 | **Writing Parenthetical Citations for Your Paper**

Change each temporary citation in your draft to its proper form. When you write your citations in your draft, check the placement, content, and punctuation of each citation.

Works Cited List or Bibliography

☑ **Prepare your Works Cited list, an alphabetical list of all the sources you have referred to in your paper. Place the Works Cited list at the end of your research paper.**

The entries in this section follow the MLA style for documenting sources, which is the style most often required by high school and college teachers. Be sure to follow exactly the style of documentation your teacher requires.

Arrange entries in the Works Cited list alphabetically, and follow the style shown on page 104.

The style for entries in the Works Cited list is exactly the same as the style you used for bibliography source cards in Step 2 (see pages 34–38). You do not have to memorize the style; you just have to know where to find it so that you can refer to it when you have a question about style.

To prepare your Works Cited list, all you have to do is to put your bibliography source card entries in alphabetical order and write them on a separate sheet of paper at the end of your research paper. The Works Cited list should contain entries for *every source you actually use* in your paper, *not* every source you consulted. Your bibliography card list will probably be much longer than your final Works Cited list.

Hint!

What if you're missing information about one or more of your sources? Page numbers? Year of copyright? City of publisher? You'll have to go back to the library or wherever you located your source and find the missing information. If you were very careful preparing your bibliography source cards, you won't have to make the annoying last-minute trip.

Instead of a Works Cited list, your teacher may require a **bibliography**, which lists *all the sources you consulted* while doing your research. A bibliography follows exactly the same format and style as a Works Cited list. Use the Works Cited list below as a model for proper form.

Works Cited   Walsh 1

"About Lacrosse." US Lacrosse. 4 Nov. 2004.
    <http://www.lacrosse.org/the_sport/index.phtml>.

Dellinger, Laura M. "Asserting Sovereignty Through Sports;
    Iroquois Lacrosse Teams Compete Internationally Using Tribal
    Passports." The Native Voice 25 Jul. 2003. sec. D: 4.
    ProQuest. Miami-Dade Public Lib. 4 Nov. 2004.
    <http://mdpls.org/>.

Fisher, Donald M. Lacrosse: A History of the Game. Baltimore:
    Johns Hopkins UP, 2002.

Hoyt-Goldsmith, Diane. Lacrosse: The National Game of the
    Iroquois. New York: Holiday House, 1998.

International Lacrosse Federation. International Lacrosse
    Federation. 4 Nov. 2004. <http://www.intlaxfed.org>.

"Lacrosse." The Columbia Encyclopedia. 6th ed. 2001.

"Lacrosse." Encyclopedia Americana. 2001 ed.

Major League Lacrosse. 2001–2004. MLL Major League Lacrosse.
    4 Nov. 2004. <http://www.majorleaguelacrosse.com>.

Mirra, Gerald B. "American Indian Lacrosse." Whispering Wind
    31 Oct. 1998: 20. ProQuest. Miami-Dade Public Lib. 4 Nov.
    2004. <http://mdpls.org/>.

National Lacrosse League. 2004. National Lacrosse League.
    4 Nov. 2004. <http://NLL.com>.

Nicholson, Lois. The Composite Guide to Lacrosse.
    Philadelphia: Chelsea House, 1999.

Tanton, Bill. E-mail to the author. 7 Nov. 2004.

Taylor, Drew Hayden. "The Irony Hangs Thick at a Game of
    Lacrosse." Wind Speaker Jun. 2002: 5. General Reference
    Center Gold. Miami-Dade Public Lib. 4 Nov. 2004.
    <http://mdpls.org/>.

Vennum, Thomas, Jr. American Indian Lacrosse: Little Brother
    of War. Washington, DC: Smithsonian Institution Press, 1994.

"Women's Lacrosse." The Book of Rules. New York: Checkmark
    Books, 1998.

Exercise 5 — What's Wrong with Each of the Following Works Cited Entries?

Fix each entry, writing your changes directly on the text. Refer to the style for writing entries on pages 34–38.

[handwritten annotations: "header on Works Cited", "indent 2nd line every source", "alphabetical order by authors last name"]

1. Dominus, Susan, "Life in the Age of Old, Old Age" from the New York Times Magazine. February 22, 2004. Section 6, pp. 26–33, 46, and 58–59.

2. Bill Bryson. A Short History of Nearly Everything, © 2003. Broadway Books: New York.

3. Harriet Tubman: The Road to Freedom, a biography by Catherine Clinton. Boston: Little, Brown. © 2004.

4. Donald L. Barlett and James B. Steele. "Why We Pay So Much for Drugs" in Time, 2 February 2004. Pages 45–52.

5. The World Wildlife Fund Book of Orchids by Jack Kramer. © 1989, New York: Abbeville Press

6. E-mail sent from Vicki Futscher to the author. This e-mail was sent and received on December 14, 2004.

Exercise 6 — Writing Your Works Cited List

On a separate sheet of paper or your computer, write a draft of your Works Cited list. Include all the sources you have actually mentioned in your first draft. Alphabetize the sources, and list them in the proper form. Exchange papers with a partner, and check each other's lists for proper style (content and punctuation).

Exercise 7 — Checking Your Progress

Answer each of the following questions about the work you've done so far.

1. Have you double-checked to make sure that every quotation and paraphrase has a parenthetical citation? How did you decide when to give a citation and when *not* to?

2. Are you absolutely sure that each parenthetical citation provides the appropriate information and is correctly punctuated?

_____

_____

3. How many works have you listed in your Works Cited list? Is each work credited within your paper?

_____

_____

4. Are you on schedule?

_____

_____

Checklist Review

☐ Follow the style of documentation your teacher specifies.

☐ Give credit for every quotation and paraphrase.

☐ Prepare your Works Cited list. Place the Works Cited list at the end of your research paper.

Revise

It is now time to revise your first draft. If you have kept to your schedule, you should have plenty of time to do the job properly. It is important that you not rush through this critical phase of the writing process. Revising is the step that will transform a tentative, rambling first draft into a focused, coherent research paper. When you revise, you must look carefully and critically at what you have written.

Before You Start

Revising certainly does not mean just one quick rereading. You need several readings (a minimum of four or five), with time to think about problems you discover and time to come up with solutions. If you have followed the general guidelines in the timetable on page 9, you will have at least two full days for revising. Use all the time available to you. There is a lot left to do.

DO IT YOURSELF. You need to do most of the hard work of revising—evaluating your paper's weaknesses and strengths and deciding what to drop, add, and change—yourself. The approach to revising suggested in this step will help you to focus on each aspect of your paper.

PEER EDITORS. You can benefit from the feedback of peer editors at any point in the revising process. Usually, however, your first draft is so rough that it's not helpful to share it with anyone. Wait until you have revised your draft thoroughly at least once, and then exchange papers with one or more of your classmates. Read each other's papers carefully. Most of all, you want to know whether your readers understand what you are saying and whether they are confused or puzzled by any parts of your paper.

☑ **Read your paper several times, focusing on a different aspect each time.**

Revising is a complex task, and it is impossible to look for everything at once. Force yourself to stay focused on one aspect of your paper at a time. Read through once for unity, a second time for coherence. Start from the beginning, and focus on each paragraph, checking for topic sentences and adequate support. Later, you will focus on each sentence and, still later, on word choices. In Step 9 you will proofread your paper. But if you spot a mistake in spelling, punctuation, or grammar as you are revising, fix it now.

When you are revising, use the common proofreading symbols to indicate changes. Even though you are probably familiar with these symbols (∧ indicates an insert; ¶ means the beginning of a new paragraph), you will find them listed on page 123 of this book.

The Paper as a Whole

☑ **Check to see that you have met all your teacher's requirements.**

Check the length of your paper, the number of sources, the parenthetical citations, the Works Cited list, and the manuscript form (see Step 10). Unless you have met all the requirements of the assignment, you are asking for trouble. If you think your paper is running a page or two shorter or longer than the required length, talk with your teacher to see if it will still be acceptable.

☑ **Focus on the paper's unity.**

The paper as a whole and individual paragraphs are said to have **unity** when everything works to develop the main idea of the paper.

DOES EVERY MAIN IDEA IN THE BODY OF THE PAPER RELATE DIRECTLY TO THE PAPER'S THESIS STATEMENT? Your outline should help you here because you dealt with this problem when you constructed it. Check what you have written against your final outline. If any paragraphs have wandered away from the umbrella of the thesis statement, either rewrite the paragraphs to bring them back under that umbrella or delete them entirely. Stay focused on your thesis statement.

Hint!

If your paper is running long, cut back wordiness rather than support. If it is running short, go back to your notes to see if you can find additional material that you haven't used.

DOES EVERY SENTENCE IN A PARAGRAPH SUPPORT ITS TOPIC SENTENCE? When you are drafting, your thoughts may stray off course a little. It is time to delete anything that does not speak to a paragraph's main idea. (Check now, also, to see that each paragraph provides adequate support for the topic sentence.)

ARE YOU SURE IT IS ONLY ONE PARAGRAPH? Sometimes a long paragraph seems strangely unfocused because it really should be broken into two separate paragraphs. Remember to begin a new paragraph whenever you start writing about a whole new idea, and make sure that each paragraph has a topic sentence. Note how the passage that follows has been revised to achieve unity.

EXAMPLE

The American poet Theodore Roethke was greatly influenced by his childhood spent in the Michigan countryside, especially the time he passed in his family's greenhouse, observing nature. ~~Roethke, in case you haven't ever heard of him, was an American poet. He won many awards, and he died in 1963.~~ As a young boy Roethke spent a great deal of time working with his father and uncle in the greenhouse, and this seemed to impress itself on his mind. In later years, he tended to view himself and the world through green-colored glasses, seeing everything as related to and intertwined with nature. (Flowers, plants, earth, and greenhouse images appear in many of his poems.) One example of this greenhouse influence appears in the poem "The Minimal": "I study the lives on a leaf/ the little sleepers, numb nudgers in cold dimensions/ Beetles in caves, newts, stone-deaf fishes." ~~I really like the images in "The Minimal."~~ ¶A second important influence in Roethke's life was the sudden death of his father in 1923 when Roethke was 15. His father's death seemed to tear apart Roethke's sense of peace and security. Roethke's deep hurt shows in much of his poetry. Critic Robert Boyers points out one example of the father's influence on Roethke's later work:

In the poem "Otto," named for his father, Roethke recaptures the sense of pride he felt in a parent who controlled a rural environment immersed in the sounds and stinks and inconsistencies of nature. (209)

Exercise 1

What's Wrong with This Paragraph?

Revise the following passage, focusing on questions involving unity. Write your changes directly on the text. Hint: Consider breaking the passage into two or more paragraphs.

Few people realize that the snake is not always a creature to be feared. Aside from sea snakes (all of which are water cobras and highly venomous), only about one-tenth of the world's snake species are poisonous. In the United States, according to the Merck Manual, the fraction drops to about one-sixth (about 20 poisonous snakes out of 120 species). In the United States more than 45,000 people are bitten by snakes each year, but fewer than 1 out of 5 are poisonous bites, and only about 15 people die from snake bites each year (Merck 2565). In fact, many snakes do a great deal of good. "Snakes are of major importance as pest controllers because of their extensive predation on destructive mammals such as rats and mice" (Columbia 2546). They also kill wild pigs, small game in the jungle, and many harmful insects. In many localities, especially in India, the cobra, which is a highly poisonous snake, is held sacred and therefore leads an almost semidomesticated life. More than 20,000 deaths in India each year are attributed to the bite of poisonous snakes. According to Hegner, the fact that a pair of cobras has come to live

under the floor of the village temple is a good omen
rather than an evil one (125). In fact, if a cobra
decides to settle down in your house it is considered a
sign of prosperity. In Europe, white storks are also considered good luck, and people build platforms on their
roofs so storks will build their nests there (Columbia
2628). A dish of water or milk is put near the cobras'
lair each day, and no one disturbs them, for they help to
kill the rats, which are a real pest in most Indian vil-
lages. "Of course," Hegner reports, "accidents do happen,
and some people who step carelessly are bitten and die"
(126). My cousin Jerrod stepped on a black snake once,
but nothing happened to him.

Exercise 2 **Revising for Unity**

In one sitting, revise your first draft, focusing only on unity. You may want to read
through your whole draft once and then carefully reread each paragraph.

Coherence

A paper has **coherence** when the ideas are clearly and logically presented and the
writer's thoughts are easy to follow.

☑ Focus on the paper's coherence.

Check to see that ideas are presented in a logical order.
You have already thought about the order of ideas as
you planned your outline, but sometimes the actual
writing reveals an order that seems more logical. (Any
order is logical if it makes sense to the reader.) If you
are writing about a topic that has a history, you will
probably present your information chronologically,
moving from past to present and maybe on to the
future. Or you might present your ideas in the order of
importance, or moving from general to specific, or in a
problem-solution or cause-effect sequence.

Hint!

If your revisions
involve reordering paragraphs
or sentences, try reading them
aloud to see how the new order sounds.
You can use the cut-and-paste
commands on a computer to
see how your rearranged
paragraphs read.

USE DEVICES TO HELP ENSURE COHERENCE: PARALLEL STRUCTURE, REPETITION OF KEY WORDS, CLEAR PRONOUN REFERENCES, TRANSITIONAL EXPRESSIONS. You know these devices from the writing you have been doing throughout your school career. They are important because they help readers follow your thinking.

Parallel structure

The poems "Bright Star" by John Keats and ~~Robert Frost's~~ "Choose Something Like a Star" ^by Robert Frost^ both discuss certain qualities in a star that may be desirable in ^a person.^ ~~human beings.~~

Repetition of key words

Keats is much more flowery and tends to use softer, more flowing ~~words,~~ ^language^ as when he talks about a "soft fall and swell" on the "new soft-fallen waste of snow." Frost, however, is much more down ^to^ ^earth^ and ^uses^ ~~is more~~ simple ^and^ direct ^more language.^ When ~~the~~ ^Frost's^ star says, "I burn," the speaker's response is, "Talk Fahrenheit, talk Centigrade." ~~The~~ ^Frost's^ speaker asks the star to "use language we can comprehend," and that is exactly what ^Frost^ ~~the poet~~ does.

Clear pronoun references

^Frost^ ~~The poet~~ alludes to ^Keats's^ ~~his~~ star in his poem, but ^Frost's^ ~~his~~ vision of a star is distinctly his own, and in the end ^the^ ~~both~~ poets reach separate conclusions.

Transitional expressions

^On the other hand^ Frost, instead of just choosing a quality in a star that he likes, is waiting for some sort of message. ^At first^ The star will only say "I burn," but ^in the end it^ tells us that we should not only be steadfast but ^(like Keats's star)^ have a certain loftiness as well.

Here is a list of some useful transitional words and phrases grouped according to the logical relationships they suggest.

SHOWING IMPORTANCE: above all, first (second, third, etc.), last, mainly, more important, most important, to begin with

SHOWING TIME ORDER: after, at first, at last, at the same time, before, during, eventually, finally, first (second, third, etc.), in the end, later, meanwhile, next, once, soon, then, when, whenever, while

SHOWING CAUSE AND EFFECT: as a result, because, consequently, for, in effect, in the end, since, so, so that, thus, therefore

SHOWING COMPARISON: also, and, another, besides, both, in like manner, like, moreover, not only—but also, similarly, still, too

SHOWING CONTRAST: although, but, despite, however, in contrast, in spite of, nor, nevertheless, on the other hand, on the contrary, still, yet

SHOWING AN EXPLANATION: for example, for instance, in fact, in other words, specifically, that is, thus, to illustrate

 **Revising for Coherence**

Revise the following passage, writing your changes directly on the text. Compare your corrections with those of your classmates. Does everyone agree on what the problems are? Have you suggested different revisions?

> Everyone dreams, and only a small percentage of those dreams are remembered. There are many theories about what causes dreams. Some psychologists think that dreams are a window into the subconscious, an important sign of inner thoughts and buried feelings. Sigmund Freud believed that dreams represent wish fulfillments. Some insist that dreams are a forgetting process, a way to get rid of unwanted or annoying emotions. Others propose that dreams are a mechanism that enables the brain to get rid of unwanted impulses and memories. Complex networks of cells in the cerebral cortex form faulty connections. During waking hours these give rise to fantasies, obsessions, and hallucinations. When people are asleep, the cortex is cut off from its normal input and output. The lower brain sends random impulses. These cause dreams.

Read your whole paper once through for coherence. Then focus on each paragraph, and see if you can make your ideas easier to follow and understand. Insert transitional words and phrases wherever you think they will help clarify ideas.

Sentences

☑ **Focus on each sentence and on the way that related sentences work together.**

VARY SENTENCE BEGINNINGS. The normal order of English sentences is subject + verb + complement(s), if there are any. (Direct objects, indirect objects, predicate adjectives, and predicate nominatives are all called **complements** because they complete the meaning of a sentence.) This word order is built into your thinking; it is probably the way you talk. But if every sentence in your paper begins with the subject followed by the verb, your writing quickly becomes monotonous. Here are some ways to vary sentence beginnings.

Hint!

Try reading your whole paper aloud to yourself, to a partner, or to your writing group. Sometimes you can *hear* problems—awkward or monotonous sentences—that aren't obvious when you're reading silently.

✱ Begin with a **single-word modifier** (an adjective or adverb).

> <u>Certainly</u>, Henry David Thoreau's experiment at Walden Pond would have to be called a success.

✱ Begin with a **transitional expression**.

> <u>Of course</u>, one of the reasons Thoreau went to Walden Pond was to experience its extraordinary beauty.

✱ Begin with a **phrase**.

> <u>At the pond</u>, Thoreau says, he learned that as life is simplified, "the laws of the universe will appear less complex...." Stripping his life to the bare essentials, Thoreau looked inward and outward and found what he was sure was the truth. <u>To understand Thoreau's experiment</u>, we must first understand the transcendentalist philosophy of Ralph Waldo Emerson.

✱ Begin with a **subordinate clause**.

> <u>When he returned to nature</u>, Thoreau found life beautiful and full of possibilities.

VARY SENTENCE LENGTH AND STRUCTURE. In an average paragraph some sentences will be short (especially those with the ideas you want to emphasize); others will be long. You don't have to count words or tally types of sentences, but it is important to create variety within your paragraphs. Remember that sentences can be classified into four types, according to their structure. (In the following examples, main clauses are underlined once, and subordinate clauses are underlined twice.)

---

* A **simple sentence** has one main clause and no subordinate clause.

  Volcanologists are searching for a safe way to predict eruptions.

* A **compound sentence** has two or more main clauses and no subordinate clause.

  One new device analyzes gases from the plume of smoke above the volcano's crater, and it can be used from a safe distance.

* A **complex sentence** has one main clause and at least one subordinate clause.

  The inventor is a scientist who survived a sudden, violent eruption of a volcano in the Colombian Andes.

* A **compound-complex sentence** has two or more main clauses and at least one subordinate clause.

  Dr. Stanley Williams, who was taking measurements in the crater at the time of the eruption, survived, but six of his fellow volcanologists died when the volcano erupted.

COMBINE A SERIES OF SHORT, CHOPPY SENTENCES.

CHOPPY: English police officers are called Bobbies. They are named after Sir Robert (Bobbie for short) Peel. Peel founded the London Metropolitan Police. Irish police officers are called Peelers. They are also named after Sir Robert Peel.

COMBINED: English police officers are called Bobbies and are named after Sir Robert Peel, who founded the London Metropolitan Police. Irish police officers, also named after Peel, are called Peelers.

Read and revise the following passage directly on the text. Vary the sentence beginnings. Combine some sentences to vary sentence length and structure. Feel free to reword, rearrange, and generally improve this paragraph. You may want to cut whole sentences, delete words, and change words. Get together with three or four of your classmates to share your revisions and talk about your changes.

There have been some great contributors to psychology. One of these was B. F. Skinner. B. F. Skinner was an American psychologist. He lived from 1904 to 1990. Skinner was a behavioral psychologist. Skinner believed that psychologists should study human behavior. They should not focus on concepts that cannot be observed. Behavior can be shaped or learned. Skinner believed this. Behavior can be shaped with positive reinforcement. Positive reinforcement includes praise and rewards. It can also be shaped with negative reinforcement. Punishment and yelling are examples of negative reinforcement (Green and Sanford 186–87).

AVOID WORDINESS AND UNNECESSARY REPETITION. Don't fall into the trap of expressing your ideas in a wordy, convoluted way. Say everything clearly and directly.

Migrating birds face ~~all kinds and sorts of~~ **many** obstacles. ~~when they are migrating.~~ For instance, ~~one of the obstacles is a~~ lighthouse**s** ~~which may~~ confuse birds, ~~and they'll often run right into the lighthouses,~~ **which are** attracted by the**ir** ~~lighthouse's~~ light. When the Washington Monument was first built, ~~in Washington, D.C., it caused the death of~~ hundreds of small ~~flying~~ birds **died** ~~who lost their lives~~ when they crashed right into **it.** ~~the Washington Monument.~~ Migrating birds have **also** ~~unfortunately ceased to live when they have~~ crashed into newly constructed bridges and ~~brand new~~ buildings. ~~that didn't used to be there.~~

**Revising Everything
There Is to Revise**

Use all your knowledge about revising to improve the following paragraph. Work especially on the way the sentences hang together. Write your revisions directly on this paragraph. When you have finished, copy your revised paragraph on a separate sheet of paper or your computer. Compare your revised paragraph with those of your classmates.

> The book A Connecticut Yankee in King Arthur's Court, by the writer Mark Twain, tells about the story of a man from Hartford, a city in Connecticut, which is why the book's title refers to "a Connecticut Yankee." The man is named Hank Morgan. Morgan is struck on the head by a crowbar. A man named Hercules hits him with a crowbar. The two are fighting. After this happens, Morgan wakes up to find himself in the sixth century. Morgan was the foreman of an arms factory that manufactured weapons in 19th century Hartford, Connecticut. Morgan sets out to bring the civilization of the 19th century into King Arthur's Court in the sixth century. Morgan comes into conflict with an old man whose name is Merlin. Merlin is the court magician in King Arthur's Court. He also comes into conflict with the ignorance and superstition of the ordinary people who live in sixth-century England. Mark Twain's novel A Connecticut Yankee in King Arthur's Court appears on its surface to be a light and humorous adventure story. It is more than that. Mark Twain has written in this novel a parody of medieval English chivalry. (A parody is a humorous imitation.) It is also a parody of medieval English romance. It is an attack on social unfairness and political injustice. It is also an attack on human ignorance. Mark Twain also attacks human superstition.

**Revising Everything
There Is to Revise**

Here is a second revising exercise, this time with parenthetical citations. Use all your knowledge about revising sentences and about parenthetical documentation to improve these paragraphs. Write your changes directly on the text.

Critics have called Sophocles' ancient Greek tragedy Oedipus Rex the first detective story. In Oedipus Rex, Oedipus sets out to find the cause of a plague that is killing the people living in his city of Thebes. Oedipus, by the way, I forgot to tell you, is king there. Oedipus consults oracles and prophets, follows clues, tracks down witnesses and interviews them, along the way he discovers that the real mystery he must solve is his own identity. Did you know that in ancient Greece the actors all wore masks? Oedipus resists what he finds out, for his is the story of a "lost one found" (Richmond Lattimore, page 82, of "The Poetry of Greek Tragedy").

The ancient Greek philosopher, whose name was Aristotle, thought that Sophocles' play Oedipus Rex was the greatest example of tragedy (Aristotle, Poetics, page 36). The play has a hero who struggles against his horrible fate that the gods have decreed even before his birth. No matter what Oedipus and others did to avoid this fate, it follows him. Oscar Brocket says this is an important theme in the play: "man's limitation in controlling his fate." (p. 51) I won't tell you what that fate was because I don't want to ruin the story for you. According to Edith Hamilton in her book Mythology, everyone in ancient Greece knew the legend of Oedipus. You can read Sophocles' play or Hamilton's retelling (Hamilton: 256–61)—or both.

Revising Sentences in Your Draft

Read through your draft again, focusing this time on individual sentences and on the way sentences work together in a paragraph. Vary the sentence beginnings. Combine some sentences to vary sentence length and structure. Reword, rearrange, and generally improve the sentences in each paragraph. You may want to cut whole sentences or delete words and phrases.

Diction: Choosing the Right Word

☑ Focus on word choice.

Your final reading in the revision stage is one of the most important. This time you will examine word choice, or **diction**.

FIND THE BEST WORD POSSIBLE. BE PRECISE. The English language is very rich in **synonyms**, words that have almost the same meaning. Find and use the word that means exactly what you are trying to say. You can discover the different shades of meaning among synonyms and near-synonyms by checking a good dictionary.

WATCH YOUR TONE. A research paper should be written in formal standard English—that is, without contractions, colloquial expressions, and certainly, slang.

AVOID CLICHÉS. Say it your way. Do not fall into the trap of using overworked, hackneyed expressions.

Exercise 9 Focusing on Word Choice

As you revise this introduction to a research paper, focus on word choice. See if you can substitute precise words for vague terms. Revise the paragraph to give it a formal tone, replacing or omitting clichés, contractions, slang, and colloquial expressions. Write your changes directly on the text.

```
    Chances are pretty good that you probably already know
that Hamlet by William Shakespeare is a really terrific
play. But the really weird thing about the play is that
nobody knows for sure exactly what Shakespeare wrote.
That's because we don't have the original script written
by Shakespeare in his very own handwriting. Guys who are
experts on Hamlet are pretty sure that the play was writ-
ten somewhere in the vicinity of 1599 or 1600, and
there're three versions that we know about. In 1604 a
```

version called the Good Quarto was written down a couple of years after <u>Hamlet</u>'s opening night. (There's a story, supposed to be true but no one knows for sure, that Shakespeare himself played the Ghost in <u>Hamlet</u>. Remember that Shakespeare was an actor before he was a playwright.) An earlier version of <u>Hamlet</u> that guys who know a lot call the Bad Quarto is a hacked-up, messed-up version that was published in 1603, but some fools must've lost it and it wasn't found again until 1823. The third version is called the First Folio—now that's confusing, isn't it. The First Folio presents a still different version of <u>Hamlet</u> and was published in 1623. This paper will talk about how the three versions of <u>Hamlet</u>'re alike and how they're not alike—and check out some ideas about what people who know a lot think about these three versions.

Exercise 10 — Revising for Word Choice

Read through your paper one last time, focusing this time on word choice. Look for places where you can use more precise words. Eliminate contractions, colloquial expressions, slang, and anything else that detracts from a formal tone.

Exercise 11 — Checking Your Progress

Answer each of the following questions about the work you've done so far.

1. How much time have you spent revising your paper?

_____

_____

2. What, if anything, did you change when you focused on unity and on coherence?

_____

_____

3. What kinds of changes did you make in sentence structure and word choice?

_____

_____

4. How satisfied are you that this paper is the best work you can do? Explain.

_____

_____

5. Are you still on schedule? (See the timetable on page 9.) What do you need to do before you are finished?

_____

_____

Checklist Review

- ☐ Allow yourself plenty of time to revise.
- ☐ Read your paper several times, focusing on a different aspect each time.
- ☐ Check to see that you have met all your teacher's requirements.
- ☐ Focus on the paper's unity.
- ☐ Focus on the paper's coherence.
- ☐ Focus on each sentence.
- ☐ Focus on word choice.

Proofread

Peanuts Reprinted by permission of USF, Inc.

You are satisfied that the content and style of your paper are as good as you can make them. But your research paper is not quite done. Your final task is to proofread your revised draft for mistakes. When you proofread, you will focus on finding and correcting errors in spelling, punctuation, and grammar. Proofreading is much easier than revising, but it still requires your total attention.

Before You Start

You will need ready access to a good college dictionary or an unabridged dictionary and a grammar handbook or a handbook on usage. (See Appendix A, What Every Research Paper Writer Needs.) You might ask your teacher if he or she has a preference about which dictionary and handbook you should use.

E-writing Remember to use the spelling checker in your word processing program. (If you have any problems, consult the Help menu.) This tool is especially useful because it may call to your attention errors in spelling that you have overlooked or of which you are unaware. Keep in mind, however, that the spelling checker cannot perform the proofreading task for you. A computer is not— and may never be—a satisfactory substitute for a careful and painstaking reader.

By the time you get to the proofreading stage, you probably will not have the time (or energy) to read through your paper several times. Most likely you will read it through once or twice, focusing on everything there is to find during proofreading. So wait until you are awake and alert. (In other words, 3 A.M. the night before your

Proofreader's Symbols

☑ **Learn to use the proofreader's symbols.**

SYMBOL	MEANING	EXAMPLE
∧	Insert	Cels are the basic units of life.
ℰ	Delete (remove)	Plant cells have a a wall and chloroplasts.
ℰ	Delete and close up	An egg is a single celll.
∩	Transpose (switch)	Red cells blood carry oxgyen.
≡	Capitalize	all cells store genetic information in dna.
/	Make lowercase	We studied cells last year in Biology.
#	Add space	When I looked at a drop of pondwater through the microscope, I saw an amoeba.
◠	Close up space	The study of cell biolog y is called "cytology."
¶	Start new paragraph	"Wow! Look at this!" Sue yelled, peering into the microscope. ¶ "Did you ever see anything so weird-looking?" Martin asked.
⊙	Period	Cells perform many important functions ⊙
⌃	Comma	Plant cells contain chlorophyll but animal cells do not.
⌃	Semicolon	Nerve cells transmit messages muscle cells contract to make movement possible.
θ	Colon	Most cells have these three things a nucleus, a membrane, and cytoplasm.
=	Hyphen	An amoeba is a one celled organism that moves by changing its shape.
∨	Apostrophe	A plants green color comes from its chlorophyll.
∨ / ∨	Quotation marks	Your lab reports are due tomorrow, Mrs. Merckel reminded us.

paper is due is not a good time.) Proofread your revised draft; make corrections; and then print out a clean copy.

DO IT YOURSELF. Give yourself enough time to read slowly, *word for word*. If you look quickly through your paper, chances are your eyes will skip right over many mistakes. Slow your reading rate to a crawl, and concentrate. A quiet room and good lighting will help. If a word looks "funny" or sounds strange, consult a dictionary. Check punctuation, grammar, and usage questions in a grammar handbook.

Here are some proofreading techniques to try.

* Read your paper aloud to yourself. This will slow your reading and help you focus on one word at a time.

* Cover the text with a piece of paper, and read only one line at a time. Focus on each word.

* Read the wrong way—from the bottom of a page to the top or from right to left.

ANOTHER PAIR OF EYES. When you have found as many errors as you can, exchange papers with a classmate or two. A peer editor may spot mistakes you have missed.

Spelling

☑ Check the spelling of words.

Students often complain, "How can I look up a word in a dictionary if I don't know how it's spelled?" Ask a friend or relative, or use your imagination and try several possible spellings. When you track down the correct spelling, be sure to add that word to your proofreading log (see page 126).

WHICH WORD? The English language has many **homonyms**, words that sound the same but are spelled differently and have different meanings (for example, *piece, peace; write, right; it's, its; wear, where; weather, whether*). Make sure that you have used the right word in the right place. That is, make sure you have spelled a word correctly according to its meaning in the sentence.

E-writing A spelling checker stops at every word not in its dictionary (that includes most names and many other proper nouns) and sometimes makes silly suggestions. On the plus side, however, a spelling checker will catch *all* typographical errors in words contained in its dictionary, such as *youself* when you meant to type *yourself*. A more serious problem occurs with homonyms. The spelling checker will not alert you to places where you have used *it's* for *its* or *accept* when you mean *except* or *already* when you mean *all ready*. Even if you use a spelling checker, you will still have to proofread your paper carefully.

ONE WORD OR TWO? A **compound word** is made up of two or more words working together as a single unit (for example, *high school, tabletop, ice cream, attorney general, cheerleader*). Check a dictionary if you are in doubt about whether to spell such words as one word or two.

HYPHENATE OR NOT? Learn the rules for when to hyphenate compound words, and double-check in a dictionary if you are unsure. You will need to hyphenate compound numbers (*thirty-one*), some words beginning with the prefixes *ex-* and *self-* (*ex-president, self-confidence*), words ending with the suffix *-elect* (*governor-elect*), and words in which a prefix comes before a capitalized word (*all-American*).

PROPER NAMES. Double-check the spelling of all proper names (author's name, title, publisher, city) in your citations.

Hint!

Do not hyphenate words at the end of a line unless the word is spelled with a hyphen.

* Make sure you have spelled the author's name exactly the way you spelled it on your bibliography source card.

* Make sure the author's name is spelled the same way in your parenthetical citations and the Works Cited list.

Exercise 1 | **Proofreading for Spelling Errors**

Cross out every word that is spelled incorrectly, and write the word correctly in the space above it.

> REM sleep has been shone to have an important conection
> with dreams. REM, which stands for rapid eye movment,
> seems to be the sleep period when most or all dreams
> ocur. During a REM period, the subject's eyes move under
> closed eyelids, they're is a change in breatheing, and
> there are distinctive brain wave patterns. A REM period
> lasts any where from ten to ninty minutes and usually
> ocurs four to six times a night.
>
> Experiments have been conducted in which patience were
> deprived of REM sleep. Researches watched the sleeping
> patience and wakened them as soon as rapid eye movments
> were visible. Subjects deprived of REM sleep were extremly
> iritable the next day and acted as if they had recieved
> very little sleep, even though they had all had their

normal amount of six to ten hours of sleep. After five
nites in a row of REM deprivation, researchers aloud the
subjects REM sleep. One subject's first REM period, which
would normaly last about ten minutes, lasted sixty-eight
minutes. It was as if his body or mind were making up for
the lack of dream sleep on the five previus nights.

Exercise 2 — Checking the Spelling in Your Final Draft

If you have time to read your paper once through just for spelling, do it now. Be
especially careful to check the spelling of names used in your citations and Works
Cited list.

Exercise 3 — Creating a Personal Proofreading Log

If you do not already have one, start your own personal *proofreading log*, a list of
errors you have found in your work. Use the lines below, or write your log on a separate sheet of paper or your computer. Besides spelling mistakes, record other
errors you have caught in proofreading: punctuation, capitalization, grammar, and
usage. Save your log for future reference. The next time you write an essay or
research paper, review your proofreading log *before* you begin drafting and also
when you proofread.

Capitalization

☑ **Make sure you have observed the rules of capitalization.**

Start each sentence with a capital letter.

Capitalize proper nouns and proper adjectives. Here are a few examples: Willa Cather, U.S.S. *Missouri*; Cincinnati, Ohio; Norwegian salmon. If in doubt, check a grammar and usage handbook to review the rules of capitalization.

Exercise 4 Proofreading a Paragraph

Cross out incorrectly spelled words, and write the correct spelling in the space above it. Use the proofreader's symbols for capitalizing or lowercasing (see page 123).

> There are many ways to look at art, and in his poem "Museum piece," the american poet richard wilbur defines three attitudes. In the first stanza, the speaker describes the museum guards as "the good gray gauardians of art" (l.1). They are ever-present, always hoverinbg about to make sure that nothing happens to any of the valueable Museum peices. They are "impartially protective" (l.3), watching over every peace of Art with equal care, whether or not they agree with it's subject matter. Even tho they may be suspicius of the french artist Toulouse-Lautrec (l.4), they protect his paintings with as much attention as they give to anyone else's. The guards don't seem to care weather or not each peace of art is appealing to them. To them, Art is an investment, to be watched over as carefuly as one would watch over a fine car or even a pile of money. Their is certainly respect in this atitude, but no love and no feeling for beauty. The whole tone of this first stanza suggests a sort of dull reliability through the use of the adjective "gray" and the description of the spongy, comfortable shoes, useful for the guards' endlecs pacing up and down the museums hall ways.

Punctuation

☑ **Read through your paper and correct any errors in punctuation.**

Indent each new paragraph. Here is a chance to take another look at each paragraph to make sure you haven't combined two paragraphs. Remember to cover each main idea in its own paragraph, complete with paragraph indent and topic sentence.

Make sure each sentence has the appropriate end punctuation mark.

> Max Planck, a German physicist, developed the quantum theory, which suggests that light is neither waves nor particles but has properties of both ("Light" 191).

Place a parenthetical citation correctly in relation to punctuation marks.

> In The Universe in the Light of Modern Physics, Planck asserts, "We have no right to assume that any physical laws exist, or if they have existed up to now, that they will continue to exist in a similar manner in the future." (393).

Use quotation marks correctly.

> Albert Einstein, who developed Planck's theories further, stated in 1930, "The most beautiful thing we can experience is the mysterious. It is the source of all true art and science" (Einstein 39).

Exercise 5 | **Proofreading Your Final Draft for Punctuation**

As you proofread your final draft, check every punctuation mark. Ask yourself:

* Is each punctuation mark the correct one? (Be especially careful not to mix up colons and semicolons.)

* Are there unnecessary commas? (Take them out.)

* Has necessary punctuation been omitted? (Put it in.)

Add any punctuation errors to your proofreading log, especially if you have made the mistake more than once.

Grammar and Usage

☑ **As you proofread your paper, correct any errors in grammar and usage.**

Check to make sure you have written complete sentences. Avoid sentence fragments and run-on sentences. A complete sentence has a subject and a verb and expresses a complete thought. If any of these is missing, you have written a sentence fragment.

              travels
      Light ~~traveling~~ at about 186,000 miles per second.

A run-on sentence has two or more complete sentences written as one sentence. A run-on sentence may have no punctuation or only a comma separating what should be two (or even more) sentences.

      Sound travels faster when air temperatures are warm⊙
      for example, at 20 degrees Centigrade, sound travels
      about 40 ft. per second faster than at 0° Centigrade.

Check to see that each verb agrees with its subject.

      Both the whale and the dolphin communicates by means
      of underwater sounds.

Check to see that the antecedent of every pronoun is absolutely clear.

      The lens and cornea are important parts at the front
                They
      of the eye. ~~It~~ focuses light on the retina at the
      back of the eye.

Exercise 6 | **What Is Wrong with These Sentences?**

Fix every mistake you find. Then, on a separate sheet of paper or your computer, rewrite each sentence correctly.

1. Henry David Thoreau, one of americas leading philosophers
    were a freind of Ralph Waldo Emerson, the essayist and poet.

2. In 1845 Thoreau built a small wooden cabin on the shore of Walden pond and he lived their for almost too years.

3. Of course one of the reasons he went to walden pond was to experience it's incredible beauty which he describes in Walden his book is based on the very detailed journal he kept while he lived in his cabin.

4. Thoreau had deeper motives tham merely appreication of natures beauty he believed as Emerson did that nature reflects the inner self and teaches us much about life.

5. In Walden Thoreau tells of meeting a poor woodcutter who had very few material things but posessed a love of nature and was honest simple and content

6. The essayist E B White called Walden "the only book I own". White said that he kept Thoreaus book handy "for relief" during times of despair.

7. In the conclusion to Walden, Thoreau wrote, If a man does not keep pace with his companions, perhaps it is becuase he hears a different drummer Let him step to the music which he hears, however measured or far away.

8. Thoreau also wrote these wrods: "if one advances confidently in the direction of his dreams, and endevors to live the life which he has imagined, he will meet with a succes unexpected in common hours

9. Thoreau's essay "Civil disobedience," which he published in 1849 explained why he refused to pay the Massachusets poll tax.

10. Both Mahatma Gandhi leader of India's struggle for independence from britain, and Dr. Martin luther king, jr. American civil rights leader was inspired by this essay

Documentation

☑ **Check your parenthetical citations against your Works Cited list.**

* Every work you have mentioned in a parenthetical citation should have a corresponding entry in the Works Cited list.

* Every entry on the Works Cited list should have at least one parenthetical citation in your paper.

* Double-check to make sure the entries in the Works Cited list are in alphabetical order.

Exercise 7 **Proofreading Your Final Draft**

Proofread your entire paper once more, this time focusing on capitalization, grammar and usage, and documentation. Correct any mistakes you find, add them to your proofreading log, and print your paper.

Exercise 8 **Proofreading One Last Time**

Don't turn in your final paper without another round of proofreading just to make sure that no new errors have crept in as you have made corrections. Read it one more time.

Exercise 9 **Checking Your Progress**

Answer each of the following questions about the work you have done so far.

1. What kinds of mistakes did you catch when you were proofreading your paper?

_____

_____

2. Are you finished? If so, hooray! If not, what do you still have left to do?

_____

_____

3. What have you learned about yourself and your writing habits?

_____

_____

4. What will you do differently next time you write a research paper?

_____

_____

5. What are the strongest parts of your paper? What are the weakest parts?

_____

_____

Checklist Review

- ☐ Learn to use the proofreader's symbols.
- ☐ Check the spelling of words.
- ☐ Double-check the spelling of all proper names (author's name, title, publisher, city) in your citations.
- ☐ Check your paper to make sure that capitalization is correct.
- ☐ Check for errors in punctuation.
- ☐ Correct errors in grammar and usage.
- ☐ Check your parenthetical citations against your Works Cited list.

Prepare a Final Manuscript

Reprinted by permission: Tribune Media Services

Congratulations! You have kept plugging away at this monumental task, one step at a time. The hardest parts are behind you. Now you have only two things left to do: reprinting your final paper and proofreading it one last time. If you have followed one of the suggested timetables on page 9, you should have plenty of time to finish before your due date. Don't try to finish your paper the night before it is due. If you wait until the last minute, something is sure to go wrong. Allow at least two days so that if disaster strikes on the first day, you will still be able to finish on time. Check to see that the equipment (computer, printer) you plan to use is working and that you have on hand everything you can possibly need. Having a printer cartridge run out of ink or toner is a last-minute nightmare.

The Paper's Form

☑ **Follow the format that your teacher requires.**

If your teacher has not specified any special requirements, follow these standard conventions:

PAPER. Use 8 1/2" x 11" white paper. Print on only one side of each piece of paper.

PRINT. A computer's printer should produce a dark copy that is easy to read.

E-writing Choose a typeface and size that are readable, and stick to them. You are not doing desktop publishing, so do not be tempted into banner heads and fancy typefaces. Keep the text plain, simple, and neat. Find out whether your teacher wants you to use italic type for book and magazine titles, or if you are expected to underscore all titles, as in the sample research papers on pages 135–150.

DOUBLE-SPACE. Set your word-processing program to double-space, and double-space the entire paper, including all quotations and the Works Cited page.

RUNNING HEAD. On every page, place a running head at the upper-right corner 1/2 inch from the top of the page and 1 inch from the right-hand edge of the paper. The running head consists of your last name followed by the page number. (See the model papers.)

HEADING. The first page of your research paper has a four-line heading that lists your name, your teacher's name, the course title, and the paper's due date. Place the heading 1 inch from the top of the page. It is flush left (aligned with the left-hand margin) and above the title.

TITLE. Center the title above the text. If you have a subheading, be sure to use a colon. Do not underscore or italicize the title or enclose it in quotation marks.

MARGINS. Use 1-inch margins at the top, bottom, and sides of your paper.

INDENTATION. Each paragraph is indented 1/2 inch (5 spaces) from the left margin. In your Works Cited list, indent each turnover line 1/2 inch, too. Long quotations set off as blocks are indented 1 full inch (10 spaces).

HYPHENATION. Do not hyphenate words at the end of a line.

PAGE BREAKS. Make sure you have at least two lines of a paragraph at the bottom of a page and also at the top of a page. This may require some juggling and/or short pages, but do not have single words or lines sitting by themselves. (These are called *widows* if at the top of a page, *orphans* if at the bottom.)

TITLE PAGE. Usually, a title page is not required. If your teacher asks for a title page, however, follow his or her specifications for content and spacing.

GET IT ALL TOGETHER. Find out how your teacher wants you to put your paper together. A paper clip in the upper-left-hand corner is the easiest solution. Do not use a staple, pin, binder, or folder unless your teacher tells you to.

Last but Not Least

☑ **Proofread your final manuscript one last time.**
Be sure not to turn in your final paper until you have read through it one last time, just to make sure that no new errors have crept in.

☑ **Make a copy.**
Before you turn in your paper, make a copy for yourself—just in case. You have worked so hard and so long that you should have a copy anyway.

SAMPLE STUDENT RESEARCH PAPERS

The following papers use the MLA style of documentation. A Works Cited list appears at the end of each paper.

SAMPLE PAPER 1

Nardoia 1 — *Running head 1/2 inch from top of paper*

Gina Nardoia
Mr. Hugh B. Corlett
English 1, Period 2
December 9, 2004

4-line heading: Name/Teacher/Class/Due date

The History and Production of Chocolate — *Title (centered)*

Carolus Linnaeus, a Swedish botanist, classified more — *Introductory paragraph begins with attention-getting facts*
than 4,400 species of animals and 7,700 species of plants
("Linnaeus"). In 1753, he named the cacao tree Theobroma
cacao. Theobroma in Greek means "food of the gods"
(Burleigh [15]). From the pods of this rain forest tree — *Citation of a source with no page numbers*
come cacao beans, the raw material of chocolate. Chocolate
has a long history as a highly prized food. — *Thesis statement*

The History of Chocolate — *Subhead*

We owe chocolate to the ancient civilizations of the New — *Topic sentence*
World. More than three thousand years ago, the Olmec people — *History of chocolate told in chronological order*
grew cacao trees in the tropical forests of the Amazon
River valley and in the foothills of the Andes (Presilla
10). Later, the Maya (who were at the height of their power — *Author's name and page number for book in Works Cited list*
from AD 300 to AD 900) continued making tchocolatl, a bitter
drink, from the seeds of the cacao tree ("Maya").

Can you imagine a bitter, gritty chocolate drink — *Attention-getting question as topic sentence*
flavored with hot chili peppers and topped with foam? That
is how the Maya consumed chocolate ("All About Chocolate").
To the Maya and to the Aztecs after them, chocolate was a
precious drink. It was used in religious ceremonies and was
considered so important that only kings, nobles, priests,
and warriors were allowed to drink it (Presilla 14–15). — *Citation of two pages in a source*

In 1502, Christopher Columbus became the first European to sample chocolate. By that time, cacao seeds had become so valuable to the Aztecs that they were used as money. "A turkey, for example, was worth a hundred seeds. A small rabbit was worth thirty" (Burleigh [10]). Even taxes could be paid with cacao seeds.

— Topic sentence

— Specific example

In 1519, Hernándo Cortés, the Spanish soldier and explorer, came to Mexico searching for gold. Montezuma II, the Aztec emperor, served Cortés and his men chocolatl ("bitter water") in special goblets, or glasses, made of gold (Jones 6). Cortés called chocolate "the divine drink which builds up resistance and fights fatigue" (Burleigh [12]). Recognizing its value, he shipped cacao seeds to Spain.

— Events told in chronological order, with many "time words" to clarify

— Historical quote found in a secondary source

A breakthrough occurred when "an inventive cook in the kitchen of Spain's Queen Isabella I added sugar instead of hot peppers, creating a delicious brew made of roasted, crushed cocoa beans whipped up with hot water or milk, sweetened with sugar or honey, and flavored with vanilla, cinnamon, or other spices" (Beach 2). Spain monopolized the chocolate trade until about 1580. In that year, a chocolate-processing plant opened in Spain. After that, the secret of chocolate gradually spread across Europe; and the Dutch, French, British, Portuguese, and Germans started cacao plantations in their tropical colonies.

— Direct quotation from a book

Only wealthy Europeans could afford the hot, frothy, sweetened drink (Presilla 20). It was served in beautiful, specially made china cups (Beach 3). In England, there were many chocolate houses, where wealthy men went to drink cocoa, discuss ideas, and gossip with their friends (Jones

— Topic sentence

7). Samuel Pepys, the English writer, noted in his diary in 1664: "To a coffee house, to drink jocolatte, very good" (Burleigh [15]).

    In 1765, cocoa beans were exported to the American colonies, and chocolate soon became a popular drink. Twenty-two-year-old Thomas Jefferson praised chocolate as "superior to coffee or tea for health and nourishment" (Beach 3). In the United States, however, there were no chocolate houses. Wealthy Americans drank their chocolate at home. Also, "chocolate was generally marketed to the masses rather than the elite (as in Europe), with the emphasis on wholesomeness rather than sophistication" (McFadden and France 23). In this way, chocolate became popular with everyone.

    Throughout its history, chocolate had been a drink. But in the nineteenth century, there were new developments. In 1828, a Dutch chemist named Coenraad Van Houten invented a press that separated the cocoa butter (the fat) from the cacao beans. The hard, dry cakes of chocolate that were left could easily be crushed into cocoa powder (McFadden and France 16). Then in 1847, an important change occurred. An English chocolate maker, J. S. Fry, combined cocoa powder, sugar, and cocoa butter to make the first solid chocolate. Chocolate could be eaten, as well as sipped! In 1876, a Swiss chocolate maker named Daniel Peter discovered how to add milk to chocolate, and the first milk chocolate was manufactured (Jones 7).

How Chocolate Is Produced

    Chocolate may grow on trees, but it is a long, laborious process from the tree to a candy bar. Cacao trees grow in tropical forests, shaded by taller trees. They have small, five-petalled flowers that develop into long pods on the branches and trunk. David Bar-Zvi, a curator of tropical plants at Fairchild Tropical Gardens in Miami, says that a cacao tree begins producing pods when it is only 4 or 5 feet high but grows to 30 feet or more. The pods vary in shape and color. Some look like deflated footballs with bumpy skins. Others are smoother and more oval in shape. Unripe pods are green, but they change to yellow or purple-red when they ripen (Burleigh [5]).

— Personal interview with an expert; appositive identifies expert

— Factual details

Workers cut the ripe pods from the tall trees—no easy task. Then they split the pods open with a machete. Inside is a gooey white pulp covering rows of almond-sized seeds—some 20—40 seeds to a pod (Presilla 10). Workers pile the seeds and pulp into heaps and cover them with banana leaves to ferment. After about six days, the seeds are spread out to dry in the sun. Gradually, they darken from tan or white or light pink to dark brown, and then they are packed in bags and sold (McFadden and France 32—33).

— Description of a process, told in chronological order

The next steps in the chocolate-making process are roasting the dried seeds and removing the husks. Then they are crushed to a smooth paste (Presilla 18). In modern chocolate factories, other steps are added. The paste is conched (gently stirred in big machines) and tempered (slowly cooled) to increase flavor and smoothness (Jones 13—14).

— Parenthetical definitions of unfamiliar terms

The Benefits of Chocolate ——————— Subhead

Many people who eat or drink chocolate say that it makes them feel happy (Kuwana). Cortés and Jefferson believed that chocolate was not only tasty but also healthy. Over

— Source of idea

the centuries, others have praised chocolate as a cure for
all kinds of ailments. Now some scientists think chocolate
may indeed be good for you. Cocoa contains antioxidant
substances called "flavonoids." Antioxidants "may help
decrease blood pressure and improve circulation" (Olson D5).
More studies will be necessary before we know whether
eating or drinking chocolate really does contribute to good
health.

    Chocolate may also have a role to play in saving some of
the world's endangered rain forests. Cacao trees thrive
only in the moist and shady tropical forests that are
threatened by logging and farming. If this valuable crop
can be grown in shady, regenerating forests without the use
of pesticides and fertilizers, and if it can yield good
profits and wages to growers and workers, it may be possible
to make saving forests economically attractive (Bright).

    So the next time you bite into a chocolate bar or drink
a steaming mug of cocoa, stop to think about the long
history of chocolate, the people who work to grow and
process cacao beans, and the things we still have to learn
about this delicious food.

> Topic sentence in the middle of the paragraph

> Direct quotation from a newspaper article

> Topic sentence

> Concluding paragraph

Works Cited

"All About Chocolate: History of Chocolate." <u>Chocolate: The</u>
    <u>Exhibition</u>. 2002. The Field Museum. 3 Nov. 2004.
    <http://www.fmnh.org/chocolate/history_intro.html>.

Bar-Zvi, David. Personal interview. 8 Nov. 2004.

Beach, Neva. <u>The Ghirardelli Chocolate Cookbook</u>. Berkeley:
    Ten Speed Press, 1995.

Bright, Chris. "Chocolate Could Bring the Forest Back."
    <u>World Watch</u> Nov./Dec. 2001:17–28. Worldwatch Institute.
    3 Nov. 2004. <http://www.worldwatch.org/>.

Burleigh, Robert. <u>Chocolate: Riches from the Rainforest</u>. New
    York: Abrams, 2002. N. pag.

Jones, Carol. <u>From Farm to You: Chocolate</u>. Philadelphia:
    Chelsea House, 2003.

Kuwana, Ellen. "The Complexities of Chocolate." <u>Neuroscience</u>
    <u>for Kids</u> 20 Dec. 2000. Eric H. Chudler. 3 Nov. 2004.
    <http://faculty.washington.edu/chudler/nchoc.html>.

"Linnaeus, Carolus." <u>The Columbia Encyclopedia</u>. 6th ed. 2001.

"Maya." <u>The Columbia Encyclopedia</u>. 6th ed. 2001.

McFadden, Christine, and Christine France. <u>Chocolate:</u>
    <u>Cooking with the World's Best Ingredient</u>. London:
    Hermes House, 2003.

Olson, Elizabeth. "Beyond Delicious, Chocolate May Help Pump
    Up Your Heart." <u>New York Times</u> 17 Feb. 2004: D5+.

Presilla, Maricel E. <u>The New Taste of Chocolate: A Cultural</u>
    <u>and Natural History of Cacao with Recipes</u>. Berkeley:
    Ten Speed Press, 2001.

Start new page;
center title 1 inch
from top of paper

Indent turnovers
1/2 inch

Personal interview
with local expert

Date of access and
Web site URL

"N. pag." means
"no pagination"

Colon separates
title and subtitle

Article from online
newsletter

Unsigned
encyclopedia article

Book with two
authors; second
author listed
with first name
followed by
last name

Newspaper article

Washington 1 — Running head
1/2 inch from top
of paper

Benjamin Washington
Ms. Applegate
English III, Period 4
December 6, 2004

4-line heading:
Name/Teacher/
Class/Due date

Lacrosse: Yesterday and Today —— Title (centered);
colon separates
broad subject and
limited focus

If you go to a lacrosse game today, you will see a fast-
moving, rough sport that resembles soccer, ice hockey, and
football. Like hockey, lacrosse is a stick-and-ball game in
which players manipulate the ball/puck without touching it
with their hands. As in hockey and soccer, players try to
score points by advancing the ball/puck past a defending
goalie and into the opposing team's net-shaped goal. As in
all three sports, they struggle fiercely to prevent their
opponents from scoring. Like all three sports, lacrosse is
an aggressive game with teams charging up and down a field.
However, as exciting as it is to watch or play lacrosse
today, it cannot compare with the earliest games of
lacrosse played by Native Americans.

Introductory
paragraph
compares lacrosse
with three
familiar sports

Transitional word

Thesis statement

A Native American Game ——— Subhead

Imagine a game that lasts three days with hundreds,
sometimes thousands, of players racing up and down a
playing field that has no set boundaries. The field might
be as long as three miles and as wide as a mile. Play stops
at sunset but is resumed at sunrise. It is said that some
players die of exhaustion (Taylor).

Attention-getting
introduction to
history of lacrosse

We have a good idea of what American Indian lacrosse —— Topic sentence
looked like from the paintings and drawings of George
Catlin (1796–1872). Catlin documented Native American life
during his travels in the West from the 1830s to 1850s. In

Catlin's <u>Ball Play of the Choctaw—Ball Up, 1834—1835</u>, we
see a melee on the field with more than a hundred players,
some wrestling each other to the ground (Hoyt-Goldsmith
12—13). One team has used white body paint to distinguish
itself from the other team, and each player carries two
lacrosse sticks. (In <u>Lacrosse: A History of the Game</u>,
Donald Fisher notes that in the Northeast and around the
Great Lakes, players used a single long stick but that in
the Southeast players used a pair of shorter sticks [13]).

In Catlin's painting, the players wear only loincloths
with decorative tails made of horsehair attached to their
backs. They wear feathers in their hair, and their feet are
bare. According to Hoyt-Goldsmith, players wore animal
charms, such as a hawk feather or bear claw, so that the
animal's spirit would help them during a game (13).

Catlin shows the game being played in a beautiful green,
flat field with hills in the background and spectators on
the sidelines. The goalpost—a horizontal sapling tied
across the tops of two tall saplings—looks like today's
football goalposts.

Lacrosse is a traditional game that has been played in
the Americas for centuries. Perhaps it is a descendant of
the stick-and-ball games played in ancient Mayan and Aztec
cultures (Nicholson 11). The game, which the Iroquois
called <u>guh-chee-gwuh-ai</u>, "was part of the Indians' religious
beliefs. Whether Algonquin or Iroquois, Cherokee or Creek,
Sioux or Santee, all believed that the Creator gave them
the game for a special purpose" (Hoyt-Goldsmith 11).

The earliest written descriptions of lacrosse come from
the diaries of French Jesuit missionaries, who came to the
New World in the 1600s to try to convert the Native

Americans to Christianity. While living among the Hurons near Thunder Bay, Ontario, Father François Joseph Le Mercier reported that clans played a series of lacrosse games to bring good weather for the newly planted seed corn (Vennum 12).

Another reason to play lacrosse was to cure the sick. Father Jean de Brébeuf wrote in 1637:

> There is a poor sick man, fevered of body and almost
> dying, and a miserable Sorcerer will order for him,
> as a cooling remedy, a game of crosse. Or the sick
> man himself, sometimes, will have dreamed that he
> must die unless the whole country shall play crosse
> for his health; and, no matter how little may be his
> credit, you will see then in a beautiful field,
> Village contending against Village, as to who will
> play crosse the better, and betting against one
> another Beaver robes and Porcelain collars, so as to
> excite greater interest. (Fisher 17)

The American Indians also used lacrosse to settle disputes between tribes, choosing a brutal game instead of war. Fisher notes that "a contest permitted tribes to reinforce political fellowship while solving territorial disputes within the context of an alliance" (14). The winner of the game won the dispute.

Because lacrosse requires great strength, skill, and endurance, its most important use was to train young men as warriors and hunters (Fisher 13). Southeastern tribes called the game "little brother of war" (Vennum xii).

According to Oren Lyons, a member of the Turtle Clan of the Onondaga Nation and all-American lacrosse player at Syracuse University:

A reason why American Indians played lacrosse

Second reason

Colon introduces long quote

Long historical quote found in secondary source

Topic sentence; third reason

Direct quote from book

Fourth, most important reason

Contemporary player talks about why American Indians play lacrosse

Lacrosse has been in our life forever. The first
mention of it is in 1600 by one of the Jesuit
priests, talking about the game, but we were playing
it long before they were here. The first purpose of
the game is as a "medicine" game played for the
health and welfare of the people. We still do that.
It was played for the Creator, to entertain the
Creator. Any person in the community can call for a
game, and then immediately the whole society . . .
creates the game. There's a whole process to it. It's
a ceremony that requires the correct procedures and
so forth. (Dellinger)

Lacrosse has always had a spiritual element for Native
Americans. Players fasted, prayed, and underwent a ritual
purification before a game. After a game, both teams went
down to a body of living water, dipped their lacrosse
sticks into the water, and said more ancient prayers. In
American Indian Lacrosse: Little Brother of War, Vennum
writes:

The Jesuits appear to have been aware that a
lacrosse match was a highly ceremonialized religious
expression—that the players were required to undergo
ritual cleansing before and after the sport, that the
game's outcome was believed to be predetermined by
spirits, and that success or failure was attributable
less to athletic prowess than to the relative power
of the religious leaders who controlled players and
games at every turn. (28)

The medicine men, or shamans, determined when games
would be played and directed the strategies. They were
something like today's coaches (Vennum 28) except that they

Long quote,
indented and
set off; no
quotation marks

Source of direct
quote

Topic sentence

Title and author
mentioned in text

Page reference
only

Topic sentence

Source of idea

had—or claimed to have—magical powers. In fact, a lacrosse match among the Eastern Cherokee was seen as a match between each team's medicine man: "And the victory or defeat is laid at the door of the medicine man rather than that the players themselves are congratulated or scorned for it" (Vennum 28).

— Topic sentence

    Only the men played lacrosse. Women cheered their team from the sidelines and were known to whip players if they weren't aggressive enough. One Catlin drawing shows a woman with a small branch chasing a player on the field. Catlin explains that she is "'yelling and screaming' as she runs, trying to overtake her husband to remind him of all the goods they have wagered on the game" (Vennum 156–157).

— Topic sentence

    Much was at stake in a game. Players and tribal members placed bets (possessions such as a tool or weapon or article of clothing) on their own team. The winning team divided the spoils among the bettors. "Although a man might lose possessions after betting on one contest, . . . he stood a good chance to recover his losses later" (Fisher 16).

Canada's National Game

— Subhead

    Canadians popularized lacrosse and took it over (Taylor). The French in Canada had named the sport "lacrosse" because the lacrosse sticks, curved at one end, resemble the crosier, or staff, of a bishop ("Lacrosse" Americana). The Montreal Lacrosse Club, founded in 1856, made lacrosse a game for white gentlemen, who very occasionally played against their Mohawk neighbors (Fisher 25).

— History of modern lacrosse given in chronological order, with many "time words" to clarify

    William George Beers, a Canadian dentist, is known as the "father of modern lacrosse." Beers played lacrosse as a teenager and was a devoted fan and promoter of the game. In

— Topic sentence; details that follow explain why Beers is an important figure in modern lacrosse

1869, he published a book of lacrosse rules in an attempt to "stabilize the erratic nature [of the game], and eliminate the petty squabbles over technicalities that inhibited the game" (Mirra). Beers lobbied to make lacrosse Canada's national sport, and on the same day that Canada became a dominion, July 1, 1867, lacrosse was declared its official sport (Hoyt-Goldsmith 15; "Lacrosse" Columbia).

Slowly, the popularity of lacrosse in North America grew. The game reached New York City by 1868, when a New York Tribune reporter wrote, "Lacrosse may be called a madman's game, so wild it is" (Nicholson 33). Intercollegiate lacrosse in the Northeast began in the fall of 1877. Canadians who settled in the northeastern states founded lacrosse clubs in Baltimore, Boston, and Philadelphia (Fisher 57).

As lacrosse became more popular, Native Americans were prevented from competing. Oren Lyons, honorary chairman of the Iroquois Nationals lacrosse team, remembers:

> But I should mention that in 1890 the Iroquois were sanctioned against playing at all. Before that we were always part of the international games. We taught the English how to play, we taught the French how to play, we taught the Canadians and the Americans. We were quite active in the late 1800s. We had three trips to England, played in front of Queen Victoria, and they couldn't beat us so they called us professionals and wouldn't allow us to play anymore. (Dellinger)

Not until 1987 did the International Lacrosse Federation accept the Iroquois as a full member nation. When they compete in international tournaments, the team travels with passports of the Haudenosaunee Nation (the Iroquois name for their people) (Dellinger).

— Topic sentence

And slowly, very slowly, women took up the game. The first woman's lacrosse association was established in England in 1912 (Nicholson 33). British women teaching in Baltimore, Philadelphia, and New York introduced the game and formed women's lacrosse clubs. The United States Women's Lacrosse Association was formed in 1931, with the first women's championship played in 1933 (Nicholson 37).

The Game Today —————————————————————————— Subhead

Youth lacrosse is growing, with most current lacrosse —— Facts and statistics about lacrosse today
players under the age of 15. There are boys' teams and girls' teams in junior highs, high schools, and colleges throughout the United States, not just in the Northeast, where lacrosse first became popular (Tanton). According to the US Lacrosse Web site, more than 1,600 high schools have a men's lacrosse program, with more than 72,000 players. More than 15,000 high school women play lacrosse in public, private, and parochial schools. On the college level, intercollegiate lacrosse is growing for both men and women ("About Lacrosse").

Lacrosse is played internationally in more than a dozen —— Topic sentence
member nations. There are World Tournaments as well as Under-19 World Tournaments for players younger than 19. According to Bill Tanton, senior associate editor of Lacrosse Magazine, "There are [two professional] men's leagues, one for indoor lacrosse (also known as box lacrosse), one for outdoor." Indoor or box lacrosse is played in ice hockey arenas, but on artificial turf, not ice. Ten professional American and Canadian teams compete —— Names of professional teams
in eastern and western divisions: the Anaheim Storm, Arizona Sting, Buffalo Bandits, Calgary Roughnecks, Colorado

Mammoth, Philadelphia Wings, Rochester Knighthawks, San Jose Stealth, Toronto Rock, and Vancouver Ravens (<u>National Lacrosse League</u>).

The men's professional outdoor league, Major League Lacrosse, is made up of six teams: Baltimore Bayhawks, Boston Cannons, Long Island Lizards, New Jersey Pride, Philadelphia Barrage, and Rochester Rattlers (<u>Major League Lacrosse</u>). The International Lacrosse Federation is made up of fourteen full member nations (Australia, Canada, Czech Republic, England, Germany, Ireland, Iroquois Nationals, Japan, Korea, New Zealand, Scotland, Sweden, United States, and Wales) and six affiliates (Argentina, Denmark, Hong Kong, Finland, Italy, and Tonga) (<u>International Lacrosse Federation</u>).

The size of a lacrosse field and the rules and equipment are different for women's lacrosse, but the game is just as frenetic. Women do not use body checks, as men do, so there is less violence and no need for padded equipment ("Women's Lacrosse" 82–83).

Although the Iroquois team still plays with traditional wooden sticks handmade from hickory wood and carefully shaped (Hoyt-Goldsmith 22–25), most players today use titanium lacrosse sticks (Taylor).

For sports enthusiasts all over the world, lacrosse is an exciting game to watch or play. Although it has undergone many changes in its long history, it is still based on traditional values. If you've never seen a lacrosse game or played one, search for lacrosse on television or in your community. You won't regret it, for lacrosse is never boring.

Facts about women's rules and equipment

Transitional word

Source cited near information rather than at end of sentence

Concluding paragraph

Call to action

Works Cited

"About Lacrosse." US Lacrosse. 4 Nov. 2004.
    <http://www.lacrosse.org/the_sport/index.phtml>.

Dellinger, Laura M. "Asserting Sovereignty Through Sports;
    Iroquois Lacrosse Teams Compete Internationally Using
    Tribal Passports." The Native Voice 25 Jul. 2003. sec.
    D: 4. ProQuest. Miami-Dade Public Lib. 4 Nov. 2004.
    <http://mdpls.org/>.

Fisher, Donald M. Lacrosse: A History of the Game.
    Baltimore: Johns Hopkins UP, 2002.

Hoyt-Goldsmith, Diane. Lacrosse: The National Game of the
    Iroquois. New York: Holiday House, 1998.

International Lacrosse Federation. International Lacrosse
    Federation. 4 Nov. 2004. <http://www.intlaxfed.org>.

"Lacrosse." The Columbia Encyclopedia. 6th ed. 2001.

"Lacrosse." Encyclopedia Americana. 2001 ed.

Major League Lacrosse. 2001-2004. MLL Major League Lacrosse.
    4 Nov. 2004. <http://www.majorleaguelacrosse.com>.

Mirra, Gerald B. "American Indian Lacrosse." Whispering Wind
    31 Oct. 1998: 20. ProQuest. Miami-Dade Public Lib.
    4 Nov. 2004. <http://mdpls.org/>.

National Lacrosse League. 2004. National Lacrosse League.
    4 Nov. 2004. <http://www.NLL.com>.

Nicholson, Lois. The Composite Guide to Lacrosse.
    Philadelphia: Chelsea House, 1999.

Tanton, Bill. E-mail to the author. 7 Nov. 2004.

Start new page; center title 1 inch from top of paper

Article on a Web site

Indent turnovers 1/2 inch

Online subscription service

Library and date of access

"UP" means "University Press"

Unsigned encyclopedia article

Full publication information and page number not needed, only edition and date

E-mail

Taylor, Drew Hayden. "The Irony Hangs Thick at a Game of
      Lacrosse." <u>Wind Speaker</u> Jun. 2002: 5. <u>General
      Reference Center Gold</u>. Miami-Dade Public Lib. 4 Nov.
      2004. <http://mdpls.org/>.

Vennum, Thomas, Jr. <u>American Indian Lacrosse: Little Brother
      of War</u>. Washington, DC: Smithsonian Institution Press,
      1994.

"Women's Lacrosse." <u>The Book of Rules</u>. New York: Checkmark
      Books, 1998.

Online subscription service

Date of access; Web site URL

Article in a book; no author given

APPENDIX A

What Every Research Paper Writer Needs

When you write a research paper, you need three things that you cannot buy in a store or borrow from a library: curiosity, self-discipline, and perseverance.

In fact, the research paper assignment is designed to help you acquire these qualities if you do not already have them. As you work through Steps 1 through 10, pacing yourself to finish on time, you will be practicing the arts of self-discipline and perseverance.

You will need some tangible things, too, and these are easier to acquire. You will need access to an up-to-date encyclopedia, a college or unabridged dictionary, an easy-to-use thesaurus, and a grammar and usage handbook. You will probably find all these in your school or local library or in your English classroom. However, it is a good idea to have a good college dictionary, a thesaurus, and a language handbook at home, too. They will come in handy for the rest of your life.

A College Dictionary

Many people talk about looking something up in "the dictionary" as if there is only one. But there are hundreds of dictionaries of the English language in print. Some are extremely good; others are not. A good college dictionary will help you find or check all the following:

* spelling
* capitalization
* plural forms
* irregular verb forms
* comparative forms for modifiers
* word origins (etymologies)
* idioms (expressions that differ in meaning from the literal meaning of the words)
* level of usage (for example, colloquial, slang, archaic, poetic)
* usage notes
* synonyms and antonyms

* biographical entries (spelling, pronunciation, identification, birth and death dates)
* geographical entries (spelling, origin of name, location, population, sometimes a little history)

Listed below are three of the best hardbound college dictionaries available. Resist the temptation to buy or use a paperback dictionary. Paperback dictionaries have fewer entries and scanty definitions, and they tend to fall apart after minimal use. If you are buying a dictionary, be sure to buy a hardbound *college* dictionary, not a *school* dictionary for young students.

* *Merriam-Webster's Collegiate Dictionary*, 11th ed. Springfield, MA: Merriam-Webster, 2003.

This dictionary has over 225,000 definitions and more than 40,000 usage examples. It includes an 18-page style handbook and is based on the authoritative *Webster's Third New International Dictionary*. A CD-ROM of the 11th edition is also included. This dictionary is updated annually to reflect new words and definitions.

* *The American Heritage Dictionary of the English Language*, 4th ed. Boston: Houghton Mifflin, 2000.

This large-format dictionary has more than 350,000 entries and more than 4,000 illustrations and drawings. Usage notes and regional American English notes provide up-to-date information on how words are used today in speech and writing. Houghton Mifflin also publishes *The American Heritage Dictionary, Third College Edition*, a standard-sized dictionary with more than 200,000 entries and many usage notes.

* *Webster's New World College Dictionary*. Ed. Michael Agnes. 4th ed. Hoboken, NJ: Wiley, 2004.

This is the dictionary used by the Associated Press as the standard for spelling and punctuation. Unlike other college dictionaries, this one was not based on an existing unabridged or earlier dictionary. It includes an easy-to-use pronunciation key.

A Thesaurus

The word *thesaurus* (thi ´sȯr əs), from the Greek *thesauros*, literally means "a treasure." The lifetime hobby of Peter Mark Roget (rō ´zhā), an English doctor (1779–1869), was grouping words into categories. For fifty years, he organized all the English words he knew and could discover into more than a thousand different categories of words related in meaning. He published the first thesaurus—his *Thesaurus of English Words and Phrases*—in 1852.

In book form, a thesaurus is a dictionary of synonyms and antonyms. A thesaurus is useful when you are trying to think of different ways to express an idea, when you want to avoid repeating the same word over and over again, and when you are searching for the word that best fits a particular context or shade of meaning.

There are almost as many thesauri available as there are dictionaries. Some require you to use an index that lists several different categories (depending on the sense of the word you are using) where you may find synonyms in the book. These index-based thesauri are more difficult to use than a dictionary-type thesaurus, which simply lists an entry word and offers a variety of synonyms and antonyms.

There is no need to spend a lot of money on a hardbound thesaurus. Here are three good paperback versions that will serve you well.

❋ *Random House Roget's Thesaurus*. 4th ed. New York: Ballantine Books, 2001.

In this easy-to-use paperback thesaurus, more than 11,000 main entries are alphabetized (just as they would be in a dictionary) with more than 200,000 suggested synonyms and antonyms.

❋ *The New American Roget's College Thesaurus in Dictionary Form*. Ed. Philip D. Moorehead. 3rd rev. ed. New York: Signet, 2002.

This paperback combines the dictionary-style alphabetical listing and occasional larger-type entries for categories (as in the original *Roget's Thesaurus*).

❋ *Webster's New World Thesaurus*. By Charlton Laird. 3rd ed. New York: Pocket Books, 2003.

This is another easy-to-use, dictionary style thesaurus. It was written by an expert on contemporary American language.

E-writing You may have available one of the many word-processing programs equipped with a thesaurus. When you highlight a word in the text, the thesaurus suggests one or more replacements. (Suggested substitutes for *reliable*, for instance, might include *faithful*, *dependable*, *unfailing*, and *trusty*.) But a computer thesaurus is much less reliable than a thesaurus in book form. Sometimes it fails completely, as if it does not understand what you are asking it to do.

A Language Handbook

When you write, revise, and proofread your research paper, you will find a well-organized language handbook extremely useful. Unless you are confident that you know all the rules for grammar, usage, punctuation, and capitalization (and who does?), it is a good idea to have a reliable "expert" to check with. Any of the hardbound handbooks listed here will last you a lifetime.

✱ Fowler, H. Ramsey et al. *The Little, Brown Handbook*. 9th ed. Boston: Longman, 2003.

This thorough, easy-to-use handbook starts out with a section on the writing process and paragraphs. It devotes sections to grammatical sentences, clear sentences, effective sentences, punctuation, mechanics, effective words, the research paper, and special writing tasks (essay exams, business writing). There are features for ESL (English as a second language) students throughout the handbook. At the back there is a 20-page glossary of usage, an appendix on preparing manuscript, and another on writing with a word processor.

✱ Kirszner, Laurie and Stephen Mandell. *The Holt Handbook*. 6th ed. Independence, KY: Heinle, 2002.

This handbook is organized into nine parts, beginning with one on the writing process and paragraph skills. Succeeding sections deal with thinking critically, composing sentences, common sentence problems, using words effectively, grammar (with 20 pages on language issues for international [ESL] students), punctuation and mechanics, writing with sources, and writing in various disciplines.

A Book on Style

You can find dozens of books that attempt to teach the niceties of writing clear, graceful English. However, there is just one you should definitely read and— if possible—own:

✱ Strunk, William, Jr., and E. B. White. *The Elements of Style*. 4th ed. Boston: Allyn & Bacon, 1999.

This slim book (only 128 pages) first appeared in 1918. The *New York Times* calls it "as timeless as a book can be in our age of volubility." The authors give rules, examples, and sage advice on points they consider essential to good writing. The book's five sections deal with elementary rules of usage, elementary principles of composition, a few matters of form, words and expressions commonly misused, and an approach to style. The style section offers twenty-one sensible rules, such as "Avoid fancy words" and "Place yourself in the background." You can find the full text of William Strunk's original edition of *The Elements of Style* (1918) online at <http://www.bartleby.com/141/>.

APPENDIX B

Writing Across the Curriculum

You may find a research paper assigned in your social studies or science class and sometimes in other classes, too. The movement to add substantial writing assignments in classes other than English is a result of a widespread effort to improve students' writing and thinking skills. The "writing across the curriculum" movement began in the 1970s and quickly became established at all levels, from elementary school through college. Teachers in subjects other than English generally give no instruction in how to go about writing research papers. They assume that you already know all you need to know from your English classes.

Usually, an assignment by a social studies or science teacher is quite specific. Here are two examples.

Social studies. Discuss the application of one amendment in the Bill of Rights to contemporary life. Cite at least one recent case heard before the Supreme Court. Summarize the arguments of both sides in the court case, and then state your own opinion.

Biology. Discuss one example of symbiosis among plants or animals. Explain how the organisms interact and the benefits and disadvantages of the relationship to each organism.

Sometimes, a teacher will ask you to choose a topic of particular interest to you that is, of course, related to what you have been studying. In that case, you will have to come up with a suitable topic and limit it appropriately. On the following pages, you will find several lists of broad, general subjects that may help you think of a topic for a research paper. These lists may be useful when you are searching for a topic for a paper for social studies, science, or an art class. They may also help you choose a topic for a research paper in your English class.

Inquiry-Based Research

The best kind of research paper starts with a question or questions that truly interest you, questions to which you would very much like to know the answers. Such research is called **inquiry-based**. The research that you do will be satisfying because you are motivated by your curiosity, your desire to find information to answer your very own questions. Here, for example, are several questions that could be researched and developed into a paper.

Biology. In some species of birds, the males and females are exactly alike in size, coloring, and marking; in others, the males and females are quite different. Why? What theories have been proposed to explain this fact?

Government. What are the arguments for and against English-only laws? Which position do I agree with, and why?

Earth science. Why are fossils found in some areas of the United States but not in others?

Economics. After several years of state-run lotteries in (name a state), what conclusions, positive and/or negative, can be reached? In what specific ways do the lotteries benefit (and/or not benefit) the citizens of the state?

THE WRITING PROCESS. Your teacher will probably want to approve the limited topic that you chose for your paper. Once your topic is approved, you will follow the same steps (Steps 2–10) outlined in this book for any type of research paper. The writing process is the same, no matter what the subject. You will need to find sources, gather information, organize your findings, and write the first draft. You will also need to allow plenty of time to revise and improve the first draft. If you keep to a timetable and follow the steps in the text, you should be able to turn in a carefully written paper for any class.

THREE PATTERNS OF ORGANIZATION. Here are three of the most common patterns of organization for research papers in various content areas.

Comparison/contrast. When you compare two or more things, you discover and describe their likenesses. When you contrast them, you tell how they are different. You may compare and contrast writers, artists, battles and other historic events, solutions to problems, species of plants and animals—you name it. As long as the two subjects have at least one important feature in common, you can develop a comparison/contrast paper.

Problem/solution. You are most likely to write this type of paper in a social studies class. You identify and describe a specific problem, discuss one or more possible solutions to that problem (or solutions that have actually been tried), and come to some conclusion about the effectiveness of those solutions. In this kind of paper, you will use the critical-thinking skill of evaluation. You will be expressing your own judgments about what does and does not work and about which solution is the best and which solution is the worst.

Cause/effect. This pattern of organization is most likely to be useful in science and social studies. You might write, for example, on some aspect of the environment or on how national and international news (good, bad, and in between) appears to affect the American stock exchanges. You can either analyze an effect (a situation or an event) to find its various causes, or you can start with a cause and write about its effects. Causes and effects are not always clear-cut; they are often a matter of interpretation. This type of paper tends to contain a lot of the writer's own thinking and speculation.

Social Studies

Social studies covers a broad range of subjects (and classes) having to do with the study of people. All the following subjects are branches of social studies: history, government, geography, economics, anthropology, archaeology, sociology, and psychology.

PARTS OF THE PAPER. If you are writing for a social studies class, your teacher may want you to use the APA style of documentation (see Appendix C). Your paper will have a title page, an abstract (a brief summary of the main ideas covered in the paper), and an introductory paragraph. The body of your paper will be grouped under headings (such as "Methods," "Results," "Data," "Procedure," "Discussion," and "Conclusions"); and instead of a Works Cited list (MLA style) at the end of your paper, you will have a Reference List.

If you are writing a history paper, your teacher may require that you use one or more **primary sources**. These are documents written during the period you are writing about. The text of the Gettysburg Address is a primary source; so are letters written to President Lincoln and newspaper accounts that appeared at the time of Lincoln's speech at Gettysburg. (A **secondary source** in this case would be a historian's account of the importance of the Gettysburg Address or a literary critic's evaluation of the speech and its structure.) If you are writing a sociology paper, your teacher may ask you to include original primary sources such as an interview or a survey you create and conduct. Unlike research papers written for English classes, social studies papers often include figures, graphs, and tables. These are referred to in the text and included at the end of the paper.

REFERENCE SOURCES. On pages 22–25 you read about general reference sources. The reference sources listed here are specific to social studies. You are likely to find them in a public library or in a local community college or university library. They may be used for browsing, if you are trying to think of a good topic, or for research in the social studies.

> *Africana: The Encyclopedia of the African and African American Experience.* Ed. Kwame Anthony Appiah and Henry Louis Gates, Jr. New York: Basic Civitas Books, 1999.
>
> *Encyclopedia of American History.* Ed. Richard B. Morris and Jeffrey B. Morris. 7th ed. New York: Harper, 1996.
>
> *Handbook of North American Indians.* Ed. William C. Sturtevant. Washington, DC: Government Printing Office, 1978–1998.

Life Millenium: The 100 Most Important Events and People of the Past 1,000 Years. Ed. Robert Friedman and editors of *Life*. New York: Life Books, 1998.

Political Science: A Guide to Reference and Information Sources. By Henry E. York. Englewood, CO: Libraries Unlimited, 1990.

Timelines of World History. By John B. Teeple. New York: Dorling Kindersley, 2002.

Women's Studies Encyclopedia. By Helen Tierney. Rev. and expanded ed., 3 vols. Westport, CT: Greenwood, 1999.

You may find it easier—and more fun, too—to browse through stacks of recent back issues of magazines, looking for articles that suggest a topic. Try *Ebony*, *Smithsonian*, *American Heritage*, *History Today*, *Psychology Today*, and *National Geographic*. Ask your librarian for help in locating other magazines related to social studies subjects.

TOPIC IDEAS. The following general topic ideas need to be limited to a specific aspect that you can research with the sources available to you. If you find a general topic that interests you, use the limiting techniques (brainstorming, clustering, questioning) suggested in Step 1 to come up with a workable topic for your research paper.

* One event, invention, or movement that changed human history
* A Native American tribe—its culture, past or present
* Slavery in the Americas
* Racism
* Women's suffrage
* Women's issues today
* A period in history you would like to have lived in, and why
* What you would put in a time capsule
* What education was like in colonial America (or any other period and place)
* Patterns of immigration to the United States in a specific period
* The Great Depression
* The American labor movement
* Child labor in the United States; in other countries
* Minimum wage laws
* Juvenile crime/juvenile justice system
* Peer pressure
* Urban problems
* Homelessness
* People with disabilities
* Curfew laws
* English-only laws
* Census data
* Trial by jury
* Freedom of speech
* Guns in American society; in other societies
* Drug education
* Gangs
* Charities
* America's two-party political system
* Voter apathy

- Rights and responsibilities of citizens
- A Civil War (or Revolutionary War) battle
- Lewis and Clark's expedition
- Early history of your town, city, or community
- A famous American speech
- An important/influential U.S. first lady
- Milestones in U.S. public education
- *Brown* vs. *Board of Education* (or some other important Supreme Court decision)
- Cuban Missile Crisis, 1962
- An immigrant's experience on Ellis Island; on Angel Island
- Civil disobedience: Henry Thoreau; Mohandas K. Gandhi; Dr. Martin Luther King, Jr.
- The biggest problem in the world today

Science, Mathematics, Technology

In a science class, the term *research paper* may have an altogether different meaning than it does in a social studies class. Instead of a survey of information others have written about a topic, a science research paper is sometimes a detailed report of the writer's original research. This research may take the form of a single experiment or a series of experiments conducted over a long period of time.

Each year almost two thousand high school seniors submit research papers to the Intel Science Talent Search, a prestigious national competition. These students describe their original research (done under the sponsorship of a teacher and/or scientist) in one of the following categories: behavioral and social sciences, biochemistry, botany, chemistry, computer science, earth and space sciences, engineering, environmental sciences, gerontology, mathematics, medicine and health, microbiology, physics, zoology, and team projects. Judges award more than $300,000 in college scholarships to finalists based on their evaluation of students' use of scientific method, experimental procedures, and detail and accuracy of data presented. For an application, rules and regulations, and directions for writing a science research paper for this contest, see the Web site of Intel Science Talent Search (www.sciserv.org/sts/). You can also find out about summer programs and internships throughout the United States for high school students interested in science, mathematics, and engineering by clicking on "Science Training Programs" on the Science Service home page (www.sciserv.org).

Find out from your teacher if there are local or state competitions that you can enter. An extremely useful resource for students entering science competitions is *Students and Research: Practical Strategies for Science Classrooms and Competitions*. By Julia Cothron, Ronald N. Giese, and Richard J. Rezba. 3rd ed. Dubuque, IA: Kendall/Hunt Publishing, 2000.

PARTS OF A PAPER REPORTING ORIGINAL RESEARCH. In many respects the parts of a science paper resemble the parts of a social studies paper. It has a title page and an abstract that summarizes in a page or less the research project or problem, poses the hypothesis (theory), the methods of research, and the results. The introduction includes a brief "review of the literature" (background information necessary to understand your project, including a summary of the most important and/or recent work on the specific topic).

The introduction is followed by a section on the experimental design (sometimes called "Methods and Materials") of your project. This needs to be detailed enough so that someone can repeat your study to see if the results are the same. Then comes a section on procedure (what you did, how you did it, how you measured it), followed by a section on your results, including tables of data, charts, and graphs, as well as paragraphs in the text describing your results. Finally there is a section on your conclusions: the purpose of your experiment, your major findings, whether or not the findings support your hypothesis, and possible explanations for your findings. At the end there is a list of works consulted in writing your paper.

REFERENCE SOURCES. Here are some reference sources you may use both for browsing, if you are trying to think of a good topic, and for research.

American Men and Women of Science. 22nd ed. Farmington Hills, MI: Gale, 2004.

CRC Concise Encyclopedia of Mathematics. Eric W. Weisstein. 2nd ed. Boca Raton: CRC Press, 2002.

Environmental Viewpoints: Selected Essays and Excerpts on Environmental Issues. Ed. Marie Lazzari. 3rd ed. Farmington Hills, MI: Gale, 1994.

Gale Encyclopedia of Science. Ed. K. Lee Lerner. 3rd ed. 6 vols. Farmington Hills, MI: Gale, 2003.

McGraw-Hill Encyclopedia of Science & Technology. 9th ed. 20 vols. New York: McGraw, 2002.

Van Nostrand's Scientific Encyclopedia. Ed. Glenn D. Considine. 9th ed. 2 vols. New York: Wiley, 2002.

Ultimate Visual Dictionary of Science. New York: Dorling Kindersley, 1998.

If you enjoy leafing through magazines, try recent and back issues of these: *American Scientist, Audubon, Natural History, Nature, Science News, Scientific American*, and *Sierra: The Magazine of the Sierra Club*.

TOPIC IDEAS. Here are some general topic ideas.

* The single most important invention of the 20th century; what life would be like without it
* Predicting natural disasters
* Do animals feel and/or think?
* Animal communication
* Animal-rights activists
* Volcanoes
* Preventable deaths
* Endangered environments/species
* Black holes

* Patents/copyrights for scientific discoveries
* Which is more important: nature (genes) or nurture (environment)?
* Benefits of exercise
* Protecting children from accidents and hazards
* Tobacco, alcohol, and other drugs
* Ethical issues in research with human subjects
* Cell biology—latest research
* Math puzzles
* Probability
* Math as a tool
* Catalysts
* Global warming
* Life elsewhere in the universe?
* What's new in the solar system?
* An organism's responses to external stimuli
* Population growth
* DNA
* Gene therapy
* Newly discovered viruses
* Underwater research
* Hybrid cars
* Acupuncture
* Herbal medicine
* Industrial robots
* Computer software
* Internet issues
* Training of U.S. astronauts
* Fossil fuels—Are the world's resources running out?
* Andromeda galaxy
* Comets and asteroids
* $E = mc^2$
* Galileo Galilei
* Gravity
* History of the periodic table of the elements
* Light: What it is, how it works
* Mars (or any other planet)
* Solar and lunar eclipses
* Space telescopes
* Quantum mechanics
* Einstein's theory of relativity
* Sunspots
* Aurora borealis (Northern lights)
* Life on a coral reef
* Earthquakes
* Hurricanes
* What fossils tell us
* Ice Ages
* Radioactive dating
* Tornadoes
* Dinosaurs
* Metamorphosis: life cycles with radical change
* James D. Watson and Francis H. C. Crick
* Asthma
* Blood types
* Colorblindness
* Vitamins: What they do; why you need them
* Braille
* Rachel Carson and DDT
* Life on a space station

Literature, Music, Art

When you write a research paper for a humanities (as literature, music, and all the arts are called collectively) class, you will use the MLA format and the MLA style of documentation. You will follow Steps 1 through 10 of the text.

REFERENCE SOURCES. Here are some reference sources you may use both for browsing, if you are trying to think of a good topic, and for research.

The American Humanities Index. Troy, NY: Whitson, 1918–present.

Benét's Reader's Encyclopedia. Ed. Bruce Murphy. 4th ed.
  New York: HarperCollins, 1996.

Contemporary Authors. Farmington Hills, MI: Gale, 1962–present.

Contemporary Literary Criticism. Farmington Hills, MI: Gale, 1973–present.

The Dance Handbook. Ed. Allen Robertson and Donald Hutera. New York:
  Macmillan, 1990.

Dictionary of Literary Biography (series). Farmington Hills, MI: Gale,
  1978–present.

Encyclopedia of Pop, Rock, and Soul. Ed. Irwin Stambler. New York: St. Martin,
  1989.

Gardner's Art Through the Ages. Ed. Fred S. Kleiner et al. 12th ed. Belmont, CA:
  Wadsworth, 2004.

The New Grove Dictionary of Music and Musicians. Ed. Stanley Sadie and John
  Tyrrell. 2nd ed. New York: Oxford UP, 2004.

The Oxford Companion to Music. Ed. Alison Latham. Rev. ed. New York: Oxford
  UP, 2002.

Magazines and journals that may be available in your library include *American Art Journal*, *American Music*, *Art & Antiques*, *Art in America*, *Architectural Digest*, *Dance Magazine*, *The New Yorker*.

TOPIC IDEAS. Here are some general topic ideas.

* Importance of one artist
* Compare/contrast two artists
* Harlem Renaissance
* Imagists (the movement in American poetry)
* American Romanticism (Realism/Naturalism/Regionalism)—movements in American literature

* Rock and roll
* Reggae (or any other type of music)
* WPA (Works Progress Administration) during the Great Depression
* Analysis and evaluation of a literary work
* Analysis and evaluation of a specific painting, sculpture

* Eastern music
* Folk art/music/dance
* French Impressionists
* Batik (or any other art process)
* Depression glass
* *Animal Farm* by George Orwell
* History of the skyscraper
* Marian Anderson's life and work
* Milestones in photography
* Diego Rivera's murals
* George Eliot's life and work
* The fables of Aesop
* Totem poles
* The life and work of Jacob and Wilhelm Grimm, the "Brothers Grimm"
* Anime
* Invention of the alphabet
* The legend of King Arthur
* Emily Dickinson's life and poetry
* Origins of theater—ancient Greek theater

* John Henry (or any other American folk hero)
* Chaucer's *Canterbury Tales*
* Hans Christian Andersen's life and work
* *Don Quixote* by Miguel de Cervantes
* Franz Kafka's life and work
* *Gulliver's Travels* by Jonathan Swift
* The work of Frank Lloyd Wright (or any other architect)
* Homer's *The Iliad* (or *The Odyssey*)
* Louis Armstrong's life and work
* Jonathan Swift and "A Modest Proposal"
* Mark Twain's life and work
* Lewis Carroll and *Alice's Adventures in Wonderland*
* Sophocles' Oedipus trilogy
* The works of Dr. Seuss (Theodor Seuss Geisel)

APA Style; Footnotes and Endnotes

Throughout this book, we have used the MLA (Modern Language Association) style of documenting sources because it is the style that most English teachers prefer. It is, however, not the *only* style. If you are writing a research paper for a social studies or science class, your teacher may ask you to use the APA (American Psychological Association) style. Or you may be asked to document your sources with footnotes or endnotes. On the following pages, you will find rules and examples for each of these methods of documentation, as used in a student paper on the Cuban Missile Crisis.

Hint!

Be sure to find out which style your teacher requires *before* you begin taking notes (Step 3). All your source citations should follow the style rules and format *exactly*. Even a misplaced or missing comma or period may affect your grade.

APA Style

The APA style is described in great detail in the *Publication Manual of the American Psychological Association* (2001). It is the style required for writers of college-level psychology and other social science papers and journal articles. It is also a style frequently used to report original research.

An APA-style paper has several elements that an MLA paper does not have:

1. It always has a title page. Centered on the title page are the paper's title, the writer's name, the course name, the instructor's name, and the date the paper is being submitted. A key phrase from the title appears as the running head on the upper right-hand corner of every page. The same phrase is centered toward the bottom of the title page. Pages are numbered, starting with 1 for the title page.

2. It always has an **abstract**, a concise summary of the main ideas covered in the paper. The abstract appears on its own page, after the title page and before the text of the paper. Often the abstract is one long paragraph; its first sentence is *not* indented. The word *Abstract* is centered at the top margin (one inch from the top of the page).

3. The text of the paper begins on the page following the Abstract page. The text is double-spaced, and each paragraph is indented. The paper's full title is centered at the top of the page. An introductory paragraph, which is not labeled with a heading, briefly introduces the topic of the paper and any findings or conclusions. Other sections of the paper may have headings, such as "Methods" (or "Methodology"), "Results," "Data," "Procedure," "Discussion," "Conclusions."

Abstract

The Cuban Missile Crisis of October 16—28, 1962, threatened nuclear war but ended as an opportunity for peace. On October 16, President Kennedy received word that Soviets were building offensive missile bases in Cuba. Kennedy and his advisors spent six days deliberating what action to take. The public was not informed of the crisis until the evening of October 22, when Kennedy addressed the nation and announced a U.S. quarantine (blockade) of Cuba. After several tense days, during which nuclear war seemed a real possibility, Soviet Premier Nikita Khrushchev withdrew the missiles from Cuba. One result of the missile crisis was that Kennedy's popularity and power grew, although some conservatives criticized him for not taking stronger or earlier action against the Soviets in Cuba. The crisis was seen as a tremendous victory for the United States in the Cold War. It also spotlighted the fear of the real possibility of nuclear war. Another result of the crisis was the realization that direct communication and negotiation between the United States and the Soviet Union were essential to world peace. American responses to the crisis reflected our concern with how our allies perceived us. In deciding to take a tough stance, Kennedy and his advisors drew on lessons learned from World War II. Two positive and lasting results of the Cuban Missile Crisis are the Limited Nuclear Test Ban Treaty of 1963 and the hotline established between the White House and the Kremlin.

4. Following the text is a **References** page or **Reference List**. It is an alphabetical list of all works cited in the text of the paper. Here are the APA rules for listing sources on the References page.

* Center the heading ("References" or "Reference List") two inches from the top of the page. Skip four spaces before the first entry.

* Double-space all entries. Use a **hanging indent**; that is, start the first line at the left margin, and indent all turnover lines for the same entry three spaces. (See the examples on page 167.)

* Alphabetize all entries by author's last name. If the author is unknown, alphabetize by the first important word in the title (not the articles *the*, *a*, and *an*). Write the author's last name, followed by a comma and the initial or initials of his or her first and middle names. End the author information with a period.

* For two authors, list each, giving the last name first. Use the ampersand sign (&) between the authors' names. For more than two authors, use "&" before the last author's name.

* Following the author's name, write the date of publication in parentheses. Place a period *outside* the closing parenthesis.

* Do not use quotation marks for the titles of articles, poems, or essays. Use regular type; do not underscore or italicize.

* Underscore titles of books, magazines, journals, and newspapers.

* For titles of all works cited, capitalize *only* the first word of the title and the subtitle and all proper nouns and proper adjectives. Keep all other words in the title lowercase, and end with a period.

* When citing publishers, use an abbreviated form for the publisher's name (for example, Doubleday, *not* Doubleday & Co.), but give the full name of university presses (for example, Columbia University Press, *not* Columbia UP).

If you record all the information you need in *exactly the right style* when you are writing your bibliography source cards, it will be easy to do your References page at the end of your paper. In APA style authors' first names are not listed, only their initials. The citations also differ from MLA style in punctuation, capitalization, and placement of information. In the chart on page 167, you will find a summary of the difference between the APA and MLA styles.

It is important to note that, as is the case with any editorial style, APA style changes from time to time. To make sure you are using the most up-to-date APA style, it is a good idea to check the APA *Publication Manual* Web site at www.apastyle.org.

PART OF PAPER	APA STYLE	MLA STYLE
TITLE PAGE	Always has	Optional
ABSTRACT	Always has	Never has
RUNNING HEAD AND PAGE NUMBER	Key phrase from title; page number on line below running head (flush right at top of page): Cuban Missile Crisis 1	Writer's last name followed by page number on the same line (flush right at top of page): Porter 1
SOURCES LISTED AT END OF PAPER	References page. Indent turnover lines three space.	Works Cited list. Indent turnover lines five spaces.
Book by single author	Finkelstein, N. H. (1994). Thirteen days/ninety miles: the Cuban missile crisis. New York: Julian Messner.	Finkelstein, Norman H. Thirteen Days/Ninety Miles: The Cuban Missile Crisis. New York, Julian Messner, 1994.
Book by two authors	Craig, G. A. & George, A. L. (1990). Force and statecraft. New York: Oxford University Press.	Craig, Gordon A., and Alexander L. George. Force and Statecraft. New York: Oxford UP, 1990.
Book with single editor	Divine, R. A. (Ed.), (1971). The Cuban missile crisis. Chicago: Quadrangle Books.	Divine, Robert A., ed. The Cuban Missile Crisis. Chicago: Quadrangle Books, 1971.

PARENTHETICAL CITATIONS

The APA author-date system of parenthetical documentation gives the author's last name, followed by a comma and the date of publication. When a specific page is referred to, a page number is also given. Here are two examples.

A letter writer to the Miami Herald (Schwartz, 1962) soberly warned: "John F. Kennedy will go down in history as one of this country's great Presidents—or its last—as a result of the [October 22] speech" (Sec A, p. 6). . . . In fact, "the fate of man hinges on the willingness to communicate" ("Showdown," 1962, p. 28).

> The Soviets call it the Caribbean Crisis; the Cubans call
> it the October Crisis; to the rest of the world it is the
> Cuban Missile Crisis (Finkelstein, 1994, pp. 103–104). . . .
> A Life ("Cuba," 1962) editorial proclaimed, "For the safety
> and solidarity of this hemisphere, our objective must be to
> dismantle not only the missile bases but the regime" (p. 4).

Here are the rules for parenthetical citation in the APA style.

* Enclose in parentheses the author's last name, a comma, and the date of publication.

* When there are two authors, cite both authors' last names and connect them with an ampersand. For more than two authors, give each one's last name, followed by a comma. Use an ampersand before the last author's name.

* Cite the page number(s) when a specific part of the work is referred to. Use *p.* (for "page") or *pp.* (for "pages") before the page numbers.

* When an author's name appears within the sentence of the text, do not repeat it in the parenthetical citation.

* When the author is unknown, the parenthetical citation should give the first important word or words in the title of the work enclosed in quotation marks.

PARENTHETICAL CITATIONS	APA STYLE	MLA STYLE
Book by single author	(Finkelstein, 1994, p. 109)	(Finkelstein 109)
Book by two authors	(Craig & George, 1990, p. 129).	(Craig and George 129)
Book by three or more authors	(Bullock, Stallybrass, & Trombley, 1995)	(Bullock, Stallybrass, and Trombley)
Book by single editor	(Divine, 1971, p. 154)	(Divine 154)
Magazine or newspaper article (signed)	(Robertson, 1962)	(Robertson)
Magazine or newspaper article (unsigned)	("Blockade," 1962)	("Blockade")
Encyclopedia article (unsigned)	("Munich," 2001, p. 1857)	("Munich")

Footnotes and Endnotes

Before the 1980s (when parenthetical citations were first introduced), all research paper writers used either footnotes or endnotes to document their sources. With these systems, quotations or paraphrases that need documentation are indicated by a superscript (raised) number following the quotation or paraphrase. This number refers the reader to the place where full information about the source is given. When the full documentation appears at the bottom of the page, it is called a **footnote**. When it appears on a separate sheet at the end of the paper, it is called an **endnote**.

Both footnotes and endnotes may also be used for additional comments or explanations that would interrupt the sense of the text. Used for this purpose, they are called **content notes**.

Footnotes and endnotes follow exactly the same style. The content and order of information are similar, but not identical, to the MLA style for entries on the Works Cited list. Here, for example, is one paragraph of a paper on the Cuban Missile Crisis, along with the footnotes at the bottom of the page. Notice that in the text the superscript number appears immediately following the punctuation mark.

> The crisis was almost uniformly seen as a tremendous victory for the United States in the Cold War. A November 2 editorial in Life proudly announced, "The Cuban blockade is a major turning point in the 17-year Cold War. The U.S. has dramatically seized the initiative."[6] We had taken a stand, made our position quite clear, and in the game of military chicken, the Russians jumped first. Not only was American public opinion overwhelmingly behind the President, but the U.S. got the support of its allies, including a 19-0 vote of confidence from the OAS.[7] On the other hand, "the Soviet setback in Cuba clearly diminished Khrushchev's prestige in the Communist world," and Khrushchev was seen as discredited and handicapped.[8]
>
> ---
>
> [6]"A New Resolve to Save the Old Freedoms," Life 2 Nov. 1962: 4.
>
> [7]James Reston, "Khrushchev's Misjudgment on Cuba," New York Times 24 Oct. 1962, sec. 1: 38.
>
> [8]"What Happened in the Kremlin?" Newsweek 12 Nov. 1962: 26.

GUIDELINES FOR PLACEMENT OF FOOTNOTES AND ENDNOTES

Both footnotes and endnotes

* Number the footnotes or endnotes consecutively throughout the paper.

* Place a superscript (raised) Arabic number immediately *after* a quotation or paraphrase, leaving no space between a word or punctuation mark and the number.

Footnotes only

* Separate the footnote(s) from the text of the paper with four lines of space or with a twelve-space rule from the left margin (as in the example on page 169).

* Indent each footnote five spaces. Start turnover lines at the left margin. Begin with the superscript number, *followed by one space*, and give the information in the order shown in the chart on the facing page. Be sure to follow the punctuation exactly.

* Single-space the text of each footnote. If more than one footnote appears on a page, use two lines of space (a double space) between footnotes.

Endnotes only

* Place the superscript numbers for endnotes in the text exactly as they are for footnotes.

* Document all endnotes, numbered consecutively, on a separate page or pages at the end of the paper.

* Center the word *Notes* one inch from the top of the page. Use three lines of space between this heading and the first note. Unlike footnotes, endnote entries are double-spaced.

* Indent each note five spaces. Turnover lines are flush left with the margin. Begin with the superscript number, *followed by one space*, and give the information in the order shown in the chart on the facing page. Be sure to follow the punctuation exactly.

	STLYE FOR FOOTNOTES AND ENDNOTES
Book by single author	[1] Norman H. Finkelstein, Thirteen Days/Ninety Miles: The Cuban Missile Crisis (New York: Julian Messner, 1994).
Book by two authors	[2] Gordon A. Craig and Alexander L. George, Force and Statecraft (New York: Oxford University Press, 1990) 132.
Book by single editor	[3] Robert A. Divine, ed., The Cuban Missile Crisis (Chicago: Quadrangle Books, 1971).
Newspaper or magazine article (unsigned)	[4] "The Lessons Learned," Newsweek 12 Nov. 1962: 21.
Newspaper or magazine article (signed)	[5] James Reston, "Khrushchev's Misjudgment on Cuba," New York Times 24 Oct. 1962, sec. 1: 38.
Encyclopedia article (unsigned)	[6] "Munich Pact," The Columbia Encyclopedia, 2001 ed.

INDEX